WORK AND CHANGE

LABOR MARKET ADJUSTMENT POLICIES IN A COMPETITIVE WORLD

A statement by the Research and Policy Committee of the Committee for Economic Development

Library of Congress Cataloging-in-Publication Data

Committee for Economic Development. Research and Policy Committee.
 Work and Change.

 Bibliography: p.
 1. Manpower policy—United States. 2. Manpower planning—United States. 3. Competition, International. I. Title.
HD5724.C6647 1987   331.12′042′0973   87-694
ISBN 0-87186-083-X (pbk.)

First printing in bound-book form: 1987
Paperback: $9.50
Library binding: $11.50
Printed in the United States of America
Design: Advanced Graphics, Ltd.

COMMITTEE FOR ECONOMIC DEVELOPMENT
477 Madison Avenue, New York, N.Y. 10022
(212) 688-2063
1700 K Street, N.W., Washington, D.C. 20006
(202) 296-5860

WORK AND CHANGE: LABOR MARKET ADJUSTMENT POLICIES IN A COMPETITIVE WORLD

Table of Contents

RESPONSIBILITY FOR CED STATEMENTS ON NATIONAL POLICY

The Commitee for Economic Development is an independent research and educational organization of over two hundred business executives and educators. CED is nonprofit, nonpartisan, and nonpolitical. Its purpose is to propose policies that will help to bring about steady economic growth at high employment and reasonably stable prices, increase productivity and living standards, provide greater and more equal opportunity for every citizen, and improve the quality of life for all. A more complete description of CED appears on page 67.

All CED policy recommendations must have the approval of trustees on the Research and Policy Committee. This committee is directed under the bylaws to "initiate studies into the principles of business policy and of public policy which will foster the full contribution by industry and commerce to the attainment and maintenance" of the objectives stated above. The bylaws emphasize that "all research is to be thoroughly objective in character, and the approach in each instance is to be from the standpoint of the general welfare and not from that of any special political or economic group." The committee is aided by a Research Advisory Board of leading social scientists and by a small permanent professional staff.

The Research and Policy Committee does not attempt to pass judgment on any pending specific legislative proposals; its purpose is to urge careful consideration of the objectives set forth in this statement and of the best means of accomplishing those objectives.

Each statement is preceded by extensive discussions, meetings and exchange of memoranda. The research is undertaken by a subcommittee, assisted by advisors chosen for their competence in the field under study. The members and advisors of the subcommittee that prepared this statement are listed on page III.

The full Research and Policy Committee participates in the drafting of recommendations. Likewise, the trustees on the drafting subcommittee vote to approve or disapprove a policy statement, and they share with the Research and Policy Committee the privilege of submitting individual comments for publication, as noted on page 53 of this statement.

Except for the members of the Research and Policy Committee and the responsible subcommittee, the recommendations presented herein are not necessarily endorsed by other trustees or by the advisors, contributors, staff members, or others associated with CED.

Subcommittee on Labor Market Adjustment

PURPOSE OF THIS STATEMENT

The Committee for Economic Development's primary mission is to study and make recommendations concerning the long-term economic related problems facing the nation. For a number of years, CED trustees have been increasingly concerned about the competitive position of the United States, faced with sluggish domestic productivity and growing competition from industrialized and developing countries alike. We risk our standard of living and, ultimately, our national security if we fail to restore the capability of our nation's businesses to compete successfully.

Work and Change: Labor Market Adjustment Policies in a Competitive World brings together various elements of CED's past and ongoing work on competitiveness. CED's first comprehensive look at the competitiveness dilemma was our study *Strategy for U.S. Industrial Competitiveness,* which has since been augmented by policy statements dealing with productivity, education, deficit reduction, and tax policy.

This new study is aimed at improving the flexibility of the work force and the capability of individuals to adapt to the many changes taking place in American business. Change is inevitable. As companies take the steps they believe necessary to improve product quality, increase productivity, and retain market share, jobs will be lost and workers will be displaced. It is vital that both public and private actions be marshaled to aid those adversely affected, without compromising the ability of firms and individuals to adapt to changing circumstances.

Competition has had a profound effect on the nature of work, on the availability of job opportunities, and on the ability of people to cope with change and adjust to prospects for new employment. This study devotes considerable research and attention to investigating the available evidence on how and why jobs are changing in the economy and the effects these shifts are having on people. The report concludes that while we can be optimistic about the future, we must take steps now to assure maximum flexibility both for our workers and for our firms—flexibility that can help foster strong economic growth and improvement in our nation's competitive position.

Winning the competitiveness battle should not be accomplished through permanent harm to individual workers, their families, and their communities. This statement offers one set of serious and thoroughly researched recommendations for public and private actions to improve the chances that this will not occur.

I would like to thank the able group of CED trustees and advisors who served on CED's subcommittee and particularly Frank P. Doyle, senior vice president of GE, who spearheaded this study and brought a high level of creativity to developing these public and private policy goals. We are also indebted to Project Director Nat Semple, CED's vice president and secretary of the Research and Policy Committee, for the considerable time he devoted to this project, and to the GE corporate staff, whose help was invaluable in producing this fine document.

William F. May
Chairman, Research and Policy
Committee

CHAPTER I:
INTRODUCTION AND SUMMARY

A CRITICAL CHALLENGE

The United States is poised at a critical crossroads. Challenged vigorously in markets it once dominated, the nation is determined to take the steps necessary to reposition its industries for competitive success. The question is how to do this with the maximum benefit and minimum cost to people. Nowhere are the choices more critical than in the area of employment policy.

The prospect of a well-paying job and a rising standard of living is the quintessential American dream. The realization of that dream for large numbers of individuals and families is the reason why the United States continues to be looked upon as the land of opportunity. Now that very faith in expanding opportunity is at risk in the debate over the employment effects of structural changes occurring in the economy, such as the shifts from manufacturing to services and from labor-intensive to knowledge-intensive industries. What we are in danger of losing sight of is the fact that as the United States restructures to become more competitive, "old" work is eliminated and "new" work created. Change, in other words, carries the seeds of opportunity as well as hardship.

Unfortunately, too much of the current debate over structural economic change is focused on the fear of change, and there is not enough focus on the employment opportunities being created, nor on the conditions needed to support the successful transition from old to new work. The danger is that policy makers will underestimate not only the tough competitive realities facing American companies, but also the necessity of timely action and the ability and willingness of people to benefit from change.

If that happens, policy initiatives are likely to be divided between two very different but equally undesirable alternatives. The first would attempt to slow, or even prevent, the process of change in the mistaken belief that such actions will mitigate the negative effects on people. The second would swing the pendulum too far in the other direction and deny the real problems and hardships created by change. In both cases, the challenge of providing for the transition of people to new opportunity is never actually faced.

CED's purpose in this policy statement is to focus attention on the one issue that, in our opinion, is at the heart of the public policy debate over structural change: the ability of dislocated workers to move on to new employment opportunity. Unless there is reasonable, widespread confidence in the availability of and access to new opportunities, the majority of people will remain unconvinced of the necessity for change and unwilling to support the steps required to ensure competitive success.

We need, therefore, to be optimistic about the availability of new opportunity, and, at the same time, realistic about what it will take to provide it.

CED's focus on facilitating the transition to new opportunity is further tied to our judgment that the more severe effects on people and communities come not from change that moves too fast, but from change that is made to move too slowly. Failure to reposition the nation's industries and work force to compete in domestic and world markets will eliminate more jobs permanently. It will also diminish the nation's ability to deal with the social costs of change. As a result, the most important test for any public or private adjustment proposal should be whether it eases or impedes the transition to new opportunity and whether it establishes or denies support mechanisms for workers undergoing the often painful and costly move to a new job.

The net effect on employment of structural changes now occurring will be determined by the actions that government, management, and labor take, first, to create or support the conditions for new opportunity, and second, to encourage people to move from old to new work.

PRIVATE SECTOR RESPONSE

Management remains, as always, ultimately responsible for ensuring the profitability of an enterprise. The difference now is that many of the measures that need to be taken to ensure profitability in an intensely competitive world are more likely to involve changes in the type of work done and the number of people employed. Labor adjustment policies, therefore, have to be factored into any decision taken by management to improve competitive position.

There are six critical elements around which adjustment policies in the private sector should be structured:
- **Communication** between management and labor regarding competitive realities, steps needed to improve market position, and the rewards employees can expect to receive for contributing to the success of the business.
- Employee involvement at the work level in the design and implementation of **productivity** improvements.
- **Flexible total compensation** that links wages and benefits directly to profitability and gives employees a stake in the company's performance.*
- **Advance notification** to employees, unions, and the local community of decisions affecting jobs, particularly in cases of plant closings, work transfers, or automation.
- Reorientation of **employee benefits** to lessen the penalties suffered by displaced workers moving between firms and industries.
- **Support programs** that allow people to shift to new opportunities, either within the firm when new work is being created, or outside when old work is being eliminated.

PUBLIC POLICIES

Government at all levels remains ultimately responsible for creating and sustaining the conditions for overall economic growth. Without these conditions, there would be little prospect for new employment opportunities, and government's ability to balance fairly the demands of competing interest groups would be diminished. Rapid change, therefore, poses as serious a challenge for government—particularly our form of democratic, pluralistic government—as it does for industry.

---

*See memorandum by SIDNEY J. WEINBERG, JR. (page 53.)

Public sector labor adjustment policies should seek to maximize values, such as mobility, that give the United States a distinct competitive advantage over other countries. The critical elements around which such adjustment policies should be structured are:*

- Incentives to **reemployment,** beginning with existing programs such as Unemployment Insurance (UI) and focused on encouraging reemployment for workers whose jobs have been permanently eliminated and who are unable or unlikely to find employment starting at or above their former wage.
- **Coordination** of public- and private-sector resources at the state and local levels to enable quick and effective response to plant closing situations.
- Commitment to **job training** programs tied closely to the needs of industry and structured to increase a trainee's chances of getting a job.
- Promotion of state and local **economic development** strategies to create jobs in communities affected by displacement.**
- **Educational reform,** emphasizing the skills and attitudes needed to prepare students for a changing marketplace of higher skilled, technology-based jobs.

---

*See memorandum by FLETCHER L. BYROM, (page 53.)
**See memorandum by RODERICK M. HILLS (page 53.)

CHAPTER II:
THE EMPLOYMENT EFFECTS OF STRUCTURAL CHANGE

The U.S. economy is undergoing wrenching changes as its markets internationalize and competition intensifies for more and more industries and firms. The scope and intensity of these changes have led some to conclude that America simply can no longer compete, that it is deindustrializing, and that millions of workers are being permanently displaced from the ranks of the employed. Still others have tried to argue that the labor market opportunities being created are mostly in low-paying, dead-end service jobs.

As a result, we are being encouraged to take for granted, even discount, the economy's vibrant strengths, particularly its enormous capacity for generating new jobs.

We are also being encouraged to ignore the connections that exist between the goods-producing and the services-producing parts of the economy and, therefore, to view the structural shift from goods to services as an ominous development.

In this chapter we look at the evidence of industrial decline and conclude that:

- The decline is concentrated in certain manufacturing industries which have lost both production and employment.
- Service industries, as well as some manufacturing industries, are growing.
- Overall, there are a number of important structural changes taking place in the economy, for example, in the mix of industries and occupations, and in the composition of the work force.
- While some of these changes are creating hardship, especially for workers experiencing the permanent loss of their jobs, still others are creating new employment opportunity.

This differentiated picture of decline and growth helps to explain, for example, why many displaced workers become reemployed only after making an industry or occupational change. It also explains why the most serious problems are experienced by workers who by reason of their geographic location, age, or education are unable to make the adjustment from old to new work without suffering extended periods of joblessness and substantial loss of earnings.

Although the focus of this paper is on employment, we also address the broader issue of structural changes in the economy, particularly the issue of whether or not these changes are leading to a downward spiral of living standards. Dispelling this notion of a downward spiral is vital if we are to provide a reason for facilitating the transition to new work. For why else build a bridge to the future, unless we are confident of the opportunity on the other side?

STRUCTURAL CHANGES IN MANUFACTURING

No other argument summarizes as well the fears about the future as the argument that America is rapidly losing its industrial base, a sure sign of its becoming a second-rate economic power. The evidence of this decline seems to be all around us. Plants are closing in the nation's industrial heartland, companies are taking steps to source manufactured products and components abroad, and a decreasing number of manufacturing jobs are being created to replace those that are being lost. These realities appear to underscore the fact that the United States is losing its competitive edge in industry after industry.

In reality, the evidence is mixed, presenting decline in some areas and growth in others. Furthermore, much of this decline has occurred in relative rather than absolute terms, and over a period of almost forty years. The evidence, in short, presents a complex picture of structural shifts in the economy that continue to change the relative positions of manufacturing and services industries. What these shifts mean will continue to be debated for some time since the picture is complex enough to sustain both optimists and pessimists.

CHANGES IN MANUFACTURING EMPLOYMENT

Job growth in the post-war period, for example, has occurred overwhelmingly in services (Figure 1). As a result, the manufacturing share of total jobs has declined

Figure 1

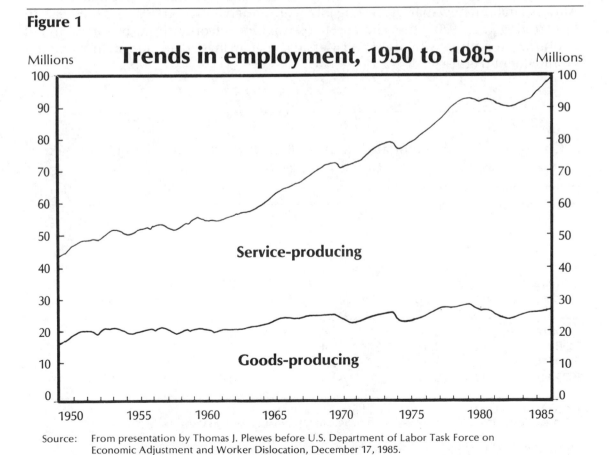

Source: From presentation by Thomas J. Plewes before U.S. Department of Labor Task Force on Economic Adjustment and Worker Dislocation, December 17, 1985.

Figure 2

Change in composition of nonagricultural employment, 1950 to 1986
(Percentage distribution)

	1950	July 1986
Total	100.0	100.0
Service-producing	59.1	75.2
Goods-producing	40.9	24.8
Manufacturing	33.7	19.1
Other (Construction and Mining)	7.2	5.7

Source: U.S. Department of Labor, Bureau of Labor Statistics.

dramatically from almost a third of nonagricultural employment in 1950 to barely a fifth (Figure 2). In absolute terms, however, the sector has more or less held its own. Almost 4 million new manufacturing jobs were added between 1950 and July 1986. In fact, during the 1970s, the United States was one of only three major industrial countries, together with Italy and Canada, that managed to add manufacturing employment (Figure 3).

Figure 3

Changes in Employment and Hours in Manufacturing, Selected Developed Countries, 1960 to 1980

Average annual percentage change[a]

Measure and period	United States	Canada	France	Germany	Italy	Japan	United Kingdom	Eight European countries[b]	Eight European countries plus Canada and Japan
Employment									
1960-80	1.0	1.3	0.6	-0.4	1.2	1.6	-0.9	-0.1	0.4
1960-73	1.5	1.9	1.2	0.5	1.4	3.0	-0.5	0.5	1.1
1973-80	0.8	0.3	-1.2	-1.8	0.1	-0.8	-2.2	-1.5	-1.3

a. Computed from the least-squares trend of the logarithms of the index numbers.
b. France, Germany, Italy, United Kingdom, Belgium, Denmark, Netherlands, and Sweden.

Source: Robert D. Lawrence, *Can America Compete?*, The Brookings Institution, 1984, p. 18.

These modest gains, however, were reversed in the early 1980s as two consecutive recessions combined with broader competitive developments in the more traditional capital-intensive industries like steel, auto, and textiles to take their toll of manufacturing jobs. By the end of 1985, jobs in this sector were about 1 million below the 1981 prerecession peak. Even with the resumption of modest growth currently projected by the U.S. Bureau of Labor Statistics (BLS), employment in manufacturing will just top 21 million by 1995, slightly below its 1979 peak.[1]

CHANGES IN OUTPUT

Manufacturing employment is only part of the picture. Changes in output also need to be considered, not only because production determines employment, but also because of the important link to productivity. If manufacturing industries are becoming more productive (and, therefore, more rather than less competitive), then output should be growing even as employment declines. This, in fact, is what has been happening. Manufacturing output continued to rise until the early eighties, when it began to decline. Unlike employment, however, which experienced only a mild recovery beginning in 1983, output grew vigorously and by the end of 1984 surpassed its prerecession peak, setting an all-time high (Figure 4).[2]

The rise in manufacturing output, without corresponding increases in employment, resulted from productivity gains which have generally been higher in this sector than elsewhere. During the recovery that began in 1983, for example, the average rate of increase in manufacturing productivity has been 4.2 percent, compared to 0.9 percent for nonmanufacturing.[3] Most encouraging of all is the fact that productivity increases in some of the industries experiencing the biggest competitive challenges, such as steel and auto, have been above their historical averages (Figure 5).

Even in relative terms the drop in manufacturing output as a share of real GNP has been much less dramatic than the decrease in employment—less than 1 percentage

Figure 4

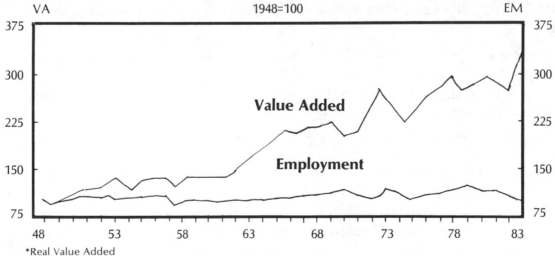

Employment and Output* in Manufacturing

*Real Value Added

Source: U.S. Commerce Department, Bureau of Economic Analysis; and U.S. Department of Labor, Bureau of Labor Statistics.

Figure 5

Productivity growth in steel and motor vehicle and equipment, annual average rate of change*

	1959-1978	1978-1985**
Steel	1.9	4.8
Auto	3.3	4.1

*Years chosen to avoid recession period and better reflect growth trend.
**1984 latest available year for motor vehicle and equipment.

Source: U.S. Department of Labor, Bureau of Labor Statistics, Office of Productivity and Technology.

point between 1973 and 1985, compared with a 6.3 percent decline in manufacturing share of total employment.[4]

The absolute increases in manufacturing productivity and output do not support the case for a rapidly eroding industrial base. Instead, they are evidence that the structural shift in the economy from manufacturing (and other goods-producing industries) to services has for the most part been a relative one and has occurred primarily in employment. Jobs in other parts of the economy, particularly services, have expanded faster as the economy overall continues to shift to areas of greater competitive advantage.

CHANGES IN PRODUCTIVITY GROWTH

That is not to say that all is well. One troubling sign is the continued decline in productivity growth since the early 1970s. Productivity is still increasing faster in manufacturing than in other sectors, but the rate of growth has slowed. Prior to 1973, manufacturing productivity grew at an average annual rate of 2.9 percent; after 1973, the rate of change slowed to 2.2 percent. The slowdown, however, has been especially pronounced in nonmanufacturing where productivity has failed to grow for the past dozen years (Figure 6). This productivity change is considered to be the principal underlying influence on the decline in real wage gains over the past decade.[5]

Figure 6

Decline in productivity growth rate since 1973, compounded annual rate of change of output per person/hour

	1947-1973	1973-1985
Business Sector*:	3.0	0.9
Manufacturing	2.9	2.2
Non-farm business less manufacturing	2.2	0.0

*Total economy excluding general government, nonprofit organizations, and private household workers.

Source: U.S. Department of Labor, Bureau of Labor Statistics, Office of Productivity and Technology.

Figure 7
Manufacturing industries with **positive** employment trend and **positive** output trend, absolute change between 1969 and 1984, and average annual rate of change,* 1969 to 1984.

Industry	Average annual rate of change, 1969 to 1984	
	Employment	Output
Nondurable goods manufacturing:		
Meat products	0.3	2.1
Canned and frozen foods	0.1	2.4
Soft drinks and flavorings	0.5	2.7
Food products, n.e.c. †	0.4	2.1
Fabricated textile products, n.e.c.	0.5	1.3
Paper products	0.1	2.5
Periodical and book printing, publishing	2.0	3.3
Printing and publishing, n.e.c.	2.0	3.2
Industrial inorganic and organic chemicals	0.9	1.4
Agricultural chemicals	0.5	2.2
Drugs	2.4	5.0
Cleaning and toilet preparations	1.4	2.7
Petroleum refining and related products	0.4	1.6
Plastics products, n.e.c.	3.7	4.9
Durable goods manufacturing:		
Logging	0.3	4.5
Millwork, plywood, and wood products, n.e.c.	0.8	3.1
Furniture and fixtures, except household	2.1	3.5
Primary aluminum and aluminum products	0.2	1.5
Fabricated structural metal products	0.5	0.2
Fabricated metal products, n.e.c.	0.9	2.0
Construction, mining, and oilfield machinery	0.7	1.5
Metalworking machinery	0.4	0.8
General industrial machinery	0.2	1.4
Nonelectrical machinery, n.e.c.	2.4	3.0
Computers and peripheral equipment	5.8	16.3
Typewriters and office equipment	0.2	5.6
Service industry machines	0.8	2.1
Electric transmission equipment	1.0	2.1
Radio and communication equipment	1.9	6.4
Electronic components and accessories	4.2	11.3
Electrical machinery and supplies, n.e.c.	1.9	3.6
Aircraft	0.3	1.3
Ship and boat building and repair	1.0	3.1
Motorcycles, bicycles, and parts	0.1	2.0
Scientific and controlling instruments	1.9	4.3
Medical and dental instruments and supplies	5.7	5.5
Optical and ophthalmic equipment	1.5	8.6
Photographic equipment and supplies	1.2	6.0

* Based on least squares trend line.
** Employment measured in thousands of jobs; output in millions of constant dollars.
† n.e.c. = not elsewhere classified.
Source: Ronald E. Kutscher and Valerie A. Personick, "Deindustrialization and the Shift to Services," *Monthly Labor Review*, U.S. Dept. of Labor, Bureau of Labor Statistics, June 1986, pp. 9-10; data on absolute changes from Valerie A. Personick, BLS.

Figure 8

Manufacturing industries with **negative** employment trend and **positive** output trend, absolute change between 1969 and 1984, and average annual rate of change*, 1969 to 1984.

Industry	Average annual rate of change, 1969 to 1984	
	Employment	Output
Nondurable goods manufacturing:		
Dairy products	(2.9)	1.6
Grain mill products	(0.1)	2.8
Bakery products	(1.6)	0.0
Confectionery products	(0.8)	3.3
Alcoholic beverages	(1.4)	3.1
Fabric, yarn, and thread mills	(2.2)	0.6
Floor covering mills	(1.1)	3.1
Textile mill products, n.e.c.†	(1.8)	2.0
Hosiery and knit goods	(1.7)	1.1
Apparel	(1.4)	1.1
Paperboard containers and boxes	(1.1)	1.3
Chemical products, n.e.c.	(0.6)	2.2
Plastic materials and synthetic rubber	(1.4)	2.3
Synthetic fibers	(2.5)	4.0
Paints and allied products	(0.9)	1.2
Durable goods manufacturing:		
Sawmills and planing mills	(0.9)	0.8
Household furniture	(0.8)	1.9
Glass	(0.5)	0.6
Stone and other mineral products, n.e.c.	(0.3)	1.6
Primary copper and copper products	(1.2)	0.1
Screw machine products	(0.6)	0.9
Cutlery, hand tools, and general hardware	(0.5)	0.4
Farm and garden machinery	(0.6)	1.0
Household appliances	(1.8)	1.5
Electric lighting and wiring equipment	(0.1)	0.7
Radio and television receiving equipment	(3.2)	5.6
Telephone and telegraph apparatus	(0.5)	5.3
Motor vehicles	(0.7)	0.9
Musical instruments, toys, and sporting goods	(0.6)	3.0
Manufactured products, n.e.c.	(0.5)	0.2

* Based on least squares trend line.
** Employment measured in thousands of jobs; output in millions of constant dollars.
† n.e.c. = not elsewhere classified.
Source: Ronald E. Kutscher and Valerie A. Personick, "Deindustrialization and the Shift to Services," *Monthly Labor Review*, U.S. Dept. of Labor, Bureau of Labor Statistics, June 1986, pp. 9-10; data on absolute changes from Valerie A. Personick, BLS.

A DIFFERENTIATED PICTURE
OF GROWTH AND DECLINE

In addition, although manufacturing output has been growing overall (with the most recent exception of the second quarter 1986), some industries are clearly in trouble, experiencing both production and employment declines. This differentiated effect is demonstrated in the following BLS breakdown of manufacturing industries into three groups over the 1969-1984 period.[6]

The first group (Figure 7) shows manufacturing industries gaining in both output and employment, particularly high-technology industries like electronic components, plastics, and computers. The second category (Figure 8) includes industries gaining in output but declining in employment, such as food processing, apparel, and motor vehicles, where demand continues to be strong, but where new or better use of technology has increased production with fewer workers. The third and final category (Figure 9) identifies industries that are losing both output and employment. These are industries with serious long-term problems, for example, blast furnaces and basic steel products, which lost 309,000 jobs or 35 percent of the total job loss for all manufacturing industries in this category.

This picture of differentiated effect is critical to understanding the nature of job displacement. Workers displaced from industries that are no longer increasing in employment are more likely to face the prospect of reemployment in new or different industries and occupations. Their successful adjustment, in other words, frequently depends on their ability to make a major job change. The higher mobility—whether industry, occupational, or geographic—required of displaced workers is an important feature which distinguishes them from the work force as a whole.

THE QUALITY OF
NEW EMPLOYMENT OPPORTUNITY

JOB GROWTH AND OPPORTUNITIES
IN SERVICE INDUSTRIES

Often overlooked in the discussion of job loss is the extraordinary capacity of the U.S. economy to generate jobs. Approximately 28 million new jobs have been created over the past fifteen years, 5.5 million since 1984 alone.[7]

Most of this increase is due to the explosive growth in the service industries.[8] Service employment has more than doubled since 1950 and has accounted for more than three-quarters of the jobs added during the current recovery. As a result, seven out of every ten American workers are now employed in this sector, while two out of ten work in manufacturing.[9]

Such growth would ordinarily be considered a sure sign of expanding opportunity, were it not for the strong doubts being voiced about the quality of service-sector employment. Service jobs are frequently and incorrectly characterized as "low-paying" and "dead-end," in other words, predominantly low-skilled jobs paying at or slightly above the minimum wage. The composition of employment growth, it is suggested, is changing for the worse as "bad" service jobs replace "good" manufacturing jobs.[10]

In fact, service-producing industries cover a broad spectrum of jobs in areas ranging from fast-food restaurants, personal service firms, and nursing homes, to computer and data processing services, legal services, and investment banking. Some of these jobs are low-paying and relatively unskilled; others are high-paying and skilled.

A similar range is found in manufacturing. As a result, not all of the jobs lost in this sector over the past decade have been highly paid. For example, textiles, apparel, and leather products, which pay relatively low wages, lost approximately 600,000 jobs from 1973 to 1985. At the same time, of course, other higher paying manufacturing industries also suffered net employment declines. Autos, for example, lost 100,000 jobs, and steel 300,000.[11]

Figure 9

Manufacturing industries with **negative** employment trend and **negative** output trend, absolute change between 1969 and 1984, and average annual rate of change,* 1969 to 1984.

Industry	Average annual rate of change, 1969 to 1984	
	Employment	Output
Nondurable goods manufacturing:		
Sugar	(2.3)	(0.2)
Tobacco manufacturing	(1.4)	(0.2)
Tires and inner tubes	(1.5)	(1.3)
Rubber products except tires and tubes	(0.9)	(3.3)
Leather tanning and finishing	(2.9)	(2.7)
Leather products including footwear	(3.1)	(1.8)
Durable goods manufacturing:		
Wooden containers	(5.9)	(4.1)
Structural clay products	(3.6)	(1.2)
Pottery and related products	(0.1)	(0.4)
Blast furnaces and basic steel products	(3.5)	(2.9)
Iron and steel	(2.3)	(1.3)
Primary nonferrous metals and products, n.e.c.†	(0.2)	(1.7)
Metal cans and containers	(2.6)	(0.6)
Heating equipment and plumbing fixtures	(0.9)	(1.8)
Metal stampings	(1.3)	(0.2)
Materials handling equipment	(0.5)	(0.6)
Special industry machinery	(0.6)	(2.0)
Railroad equipment	(1.6)	(5.1)
Transportation equipment, n.e.c.	(2.5)	(0.8)
Watches, clocks, and clock-operated devices	(4.8)	(1.7)

* Based on least squares trend line.
** Employment measured in thousands of jobs; output in millions of constant dollars.
† n.e.c. = not elsewhere classified.
Source: Ronald E. Kutscher and Valerie A. Personick, "Deindustrialization and the Shift to Services," *Monthly Labor Review*, U.S. Dept. of Labor, Bureau of Labor Statistics, June 1986, pp. 9-10; data on absolute changes from Valerie A. Personick, BLS.

Figure 10

*Total employment and hourly and weekly earnings in
service-producing industries and manufacturing, 1985 annual averages*

	Total employment	Percent of sector	Average hourly earnings*	Average weekly earnings*
Goods-Producing Sector	24 930	100%	N/A	N/A
Manufacturing	19 314	77%	9.53	385.97
Service-Producing Sector	72 684	100%	N/A	N/A
Government	16 415	23%	N/A	N/A
Private Service-Producing	56 269	77%	N/A	N/A
Transport. and Public Util.	5 242	7%	11.40	450.30
Wholesale Trade	5 740	8%	9.16	351.74
Retail Trade	17 360	24%	5.94	174.64
Finance, Insurance, and Real Estate	5 953	8%	7.94	289.02
Services	21 974	30%	7.89	256.43
Total Private Nonagricultural Establishments	81 199	---	8.57	299.09

* Production or nonsupervisory workers only.

Source: *Supplement to Employment and Earnings,* revised establishment data, U.S. Department of Labor, Bureau of
  Labor Statistics, June 1986.

Pointing out the diversity of employment in manufacturing and services, however, will not put an end to the debate over the quality of job growth in the United States. That debate will continue because of the gap between average earnings in manufacturing and earnings in many of the service-producing industries (Figure 10).

Average earnings are shaped by underlying movements in the economy. Some of these movements are having the effect of depressing earnings levels; others are serving to increase the rate of earnings growth. Our discussion so far has focused on the changes in the structure of industries from goods to services. However, other significant changes affecting the quality of job growth have been taking place simultaneously, for example, changes in the demographic mix of the labor force and in the structure of occupations.

THE EFFECTS OF DEMOGRAPHIC CHANGES

Between 1970 and 1985, the labor force expanded dramatically, reflecting both the entry of the "baby boom" generation and the increased participation of women (Figure 11). By 1985, 115.5 million people were in the labor force, an increase of 33 million from 1970. Women accounted for about 60 percent of the total growth. Their participation rate during this fifteen-year period increased by over 11 percentage

Figure 11

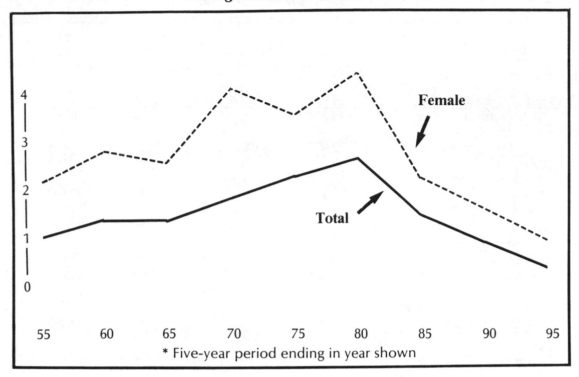

LABOR FORCE
Average Annual % Growth*

* Five-year period ending in year shown

Source: Howard M. Fullerton, "The 1995 Labor Forces BLS' Latest Projection," *Monthly Labor Review*, U.S. Department of Labor, Bureau of Labor Statistics, November 1985, pp. 17-25.

points, so that by 1985, women made up approximately 44 percent of the labor force, up from 38 percent in 1970. The prime-age work force also increased its participation rate by 9.5 points; by 1985 this group represented two-thirds of the labor force, up 6 percentage points since 1970 (Figure 12).[12]

The dramatic influx of new entrants has reshaped the composition of the work force. It also has tended to depress average earnings in the service sector where most new workers, especially women, have found employment.[13] Data on the usual weekly earnings of full-time workers, however, indicate that while the level of pay for women is below average, their pay has been growing one percentage point faster per year than the average for all full-time workers since 1979.[14] Additional data from the government's broadest measure of compensation costs show that compensation has been growing at a faster rate in the service-producing sector than in the goods-producing sector, indicating movement toward a narrowing of the gap between the two sectors.[15]

THE CHANGING MIX OF OCCUPATIONS

Another significant development affecting the quality of job growth has been the changing mix of occupations in both goods- and service-producing industries. In this case, the evidence points to a trend toward higher-than-average earnings occupa-

Figure 12

U.S. Labor Force, 1970 to 1985

	Number (millions)				Growth Rates (percent)		
					1970 to 1975	1975 to 1980	1980 to 1985
	1970	1975	1980	1985	1975	1980	1985
Total, 16 and older	82.8	93.8	106.9	115.5	2.5	2.6	1.6
Men	51.2	56.3	61.5	64.4	1.9	1.8	.9
Women	31.5	37.5	45.5	51.0	3.5	3.9	2.3
Youth, 16 to 24	17.8	22.6	25.3	23.6	4.9	2.3	-1.4
Prime, 25 to 54	50.4	56.9	66.6	76.9	2.5	3.2	2.9
Older, 55 and up	14.5	14.3	15.0	14.9	-.3	1.0	-.1
Black	—	9.3	10.9	12.4	—	3.2	2.6
Hispanic	—	—	5.7	7.7	—	—	6.2

Labor Force Participation Rates, 1970 to 1985
(Percent)

	1970	1975	1980	1985
Total, 16 and older	60.4	61.2	63.8	64.8
Men	79.7	77.9	77.4	76.3
Women	43.3	46.3	51.5	54.5
Youth, 16 to 24	59.8	64.6	68.1	68.3
Prime, 25 to 54	72.0	74.1	78.6	81.5
Older, 55 and older	38.9	34.6	32.8	30.3
Black	—	58.8	60.9	62.9
Hispanic	—	—	64.0	64.6

Distribution of the Labor Force, 1970 to 1985
(Percent)

	1970	1975	1980	1985
Total, 16 and older	100.0	100.0	100.0	100.0
Men	61.8	60.0	57.5	55.8
Women	38.2	40.0	42.5	44.2
Youth, 16 to 24	21.5	24.1	23.7	20.4
Prime, 25 to 54	60.9	60.7	62.3	66.6
Older, 55 and older	17.6	15.2	14.0	13.0
Black	—	9.9	10.2	10.7
Hispanic	—	—	5.3	6.7

Note: These data are from Current Population Survey and are the total labor force, including the resident armed forces.

Source: Ronald E. Kutcher, U.S. Department of Labor, Bureau of Labor Statistics, from "Employment Growth in the United States," presented to the National Council on Employment Policy, Washington, DC, April 17, 1986.

tions and away from occupations with lower-than-average earnings. A BLS analysis of total occupational employment in 1973 and 1982 reveals that slightly over half of the jobs added between these two years were in the professional and managerial occupations, raising their combined share of total employment almost 5 percentage points.

Most of the job losses, on the other hand, occurred largely among operatives, which together with farmers and private household workers declined both in absolute numbers and as a percentage of overall employment (Figure 13).[16]

The BLS projects that this change in the occupational structure of the economy will continue through the 1990s. Nearly 16 million jobs are expected to be added between 1984 and 1995. Much of this growth will be concentrated in five broad occupational groups, three of which (executive, administrative, and managerial workers; professional workers; technicians and related support workers) have the highest proportion of workers with a college education or specialized post-secondary technical training (Figure 14).[17]

The variety and magnitude of changes in industries, occupations, and demographics make it difficult to draw conclusions about net effects. Some of the changes point to gains (for example, the rapid expansion of employment to accommodate large numbers of new workers, the shift toward higher paying, higher skilled occupations), others to losses (the production and employment declines in particular industries, the slowdown in productivity growth). The evidence, although mixed, clearly indicates the continuing generation of new opportunity. Still unanswered, however, is whether or not policy makers have enough confidence in the process of change to facilitate the positive shifts that are already underway.

Unfortunately, much of the debate over structural change remains locked into outdated ways of thinking about the economy. The assumption that gains in one part of the economy automatically signal losses in another overlooks the growing interdependence between goods- and service-producing industries. The growth, for example, of producer services (business and repair, real estate, and finance) is closely

Figure 13

Employment in the United States by Major Occupational Group
1972 to 1982
(Thousands)

Occupational Group	Absolute 1972	Percent Distribution 1972	Absolute 1982	Percent Distribution 1982	1972 to 1982 Absolute Change	1972 to 1982 Percent Change
Total, all occupations	81 702	100.0	99 526	100.0	17 824	+21.8
Professional, technical, and kindred workers	11 459	14.0	16 951	17.0	5 492	+47.9
Managers and administrators	8 031	9.8	11 493	11.5	3 462	+43.1
Sales workers	5 354	6.6	6 580	6.6	1 226	+22.9
Clerical and kindred workers	14 247	17.4	18 446	18.5	4 199	+29.5
Craft and kindred workers	10 810	13.2	12 272	12.3	1 462	+13.5
Operatives, except transport	10 340	12.7	9 429	9.5	-911	-8.8
Transport operatives	3 209	3.9	3 377	3.4	168	+5.2
Laborers, except farm	4 217	5.2	4 518	4.5	301	+7.1
Farmers and farm laborers	3 069	3.8	2 723	2.7	-346	-11.3
Service workers, except household	9 529	11.7	12 694	12.8	3 165	+33.2
Private household workers	1 437	1.8	1 042	1.0	-395	-27.5

Source: Ronald E. Kutscher, U.S. Department of Labor, Bureau of Labor Statistics, from "Employment Growth in the United States." Presentation to the National Council on Employment Policy, Washington, DC; April 17, 1986; Distribution figures from *Employment and Earnings,* U.S. Department of Labor, Bureau of Labor Statistics, January 1973 and 1983.

Figure 14

Total civilian employment by broad occupational group, actual 1984 and projected 1995, and percent change in employment, 1973 to 1984 and 1984 to 1995

Occupation	1984		1995		Percent change in employment	
	Number	Percent	Number	Percent	1973-84	1984-95
Total employment	106 843	100.0	122 760	100.0	23.4	14.9
Executive, administrative, and managerial workers	11 274	10.6	13 762	11.2	48.4	22.1
Professional workers	12 805	12.0	15 578	12.7	46.2	21.7
Technicians and related support workers	3 206	3.0	4 119	3.4	58.3	28.7
Salesworkers	11 173	10.5	13 393	10.9	41.5	19.9
Administrative support workers, including clerical	18 716	17.5	20 499	16.7	24.7	9.5
Private household workers	993	.9	811	.7	-27.0	-18.3
Service workers, except private household workers	15 589	14.6	18 917	15.4	37.6	21.3
Precision production, craft, and repair workers	12 176	11.4	13 601	11.1	20.2	11.7
Operators, fabricators, and laborers	17 357	16.2	18 634	15.2	-7.2	7.3
Farming, forestry, and fishing workers	3 554	3.3	3 447	2.8	-5.9	-3.0

Source: George T. Silvestri and John M. Lukasiewicz, "Occupational Employment Projections: The 1984-95 Outlook," *Monthly Labor Review*, Bureau of Labor Statistics, U.S. Department of Labor, November 1985.

related to the changing needs of the mostly goods-producing industries who are their customers. The links between the two sectors will be strengthened even further as many service industries increase their capital intensity and improve productivity.[18]

JOB DISPLACEMENT AND ADJUSTMENT

Each time a manufacturing plant closes, the reality of displacement is brought forcefully home, particularly since employment in the basic industries has provided the opportunity for many American families to enter and thrive in the middle class. As a result, the misconception exists that each year millions of workers are permanently displaced from the work force, never again to become employed except perhaps in very low-paying jobs.

That, fortunately, is not what is happening. Although our understanding of displacement is very recent, what we do know suggests that the majority of workers become reemployed fairly quickly and, in many cases, earn as much or more in their new jobs. At the same time, however, sizable numbers of workers experience extended periods of joblessness and initial loss of earnings upon reemployment.

THE CHARACTERISTICS OF DISPLACED WORKERS

This picture of displacement is based on the BLS special household survey of workers who lost their jobs in the five years between January 1979 and January 1984.[19]

The BLS estimated that a total of 5.1 million workers were "displaced" during this five-year period. These were workers who had lost jobs because of plant closings or moves, slack work, or the abolishment of their positions or shifts. The BLS further limited its focus to workers who had been on their jobs for at least three years.[20] As of January 1984, 60 percent of the 5.1 million displaced workers were reemployed, 26 percent were still looking for work, and 14 percent had left the work force. Two-thirds of the reemployed workers found jobs within six months after being dis-

Figure 15

Employment status and area of residence in January 1984 of displaced workers by selected characteristics

(Numbers in thousands)

Characteristic	Total°	New England	Middle Atlantic	East North Central	West North Central	South Atlantic	East South Central	West South Central	Mountain	Pacific
Workers who lost jobs										
Total	5,091	260	794	1,206	426	664	378	484	211	667
Men	3,328	155	530	772	282	428	236	347	152	427
Women	1,763	105	264	434	145	236	143	137	59	241
Reason for job loss										
Plant or company closed down or moved	2,492	118	410	556	208	339	204	231	103	323
Slack work	1,970	106	269	513	164	236	132	211	83	256
Position or shift abolished	629	36	115	138	54	89	42	42	26	88
Industry of lost job										
Construction	481	16	68	88	36	81	34	63	30	63
Manufacturing	2,514	158	414	658	210	296	189	215	58	315
Durable goods	1,686	94	260	514	137	175	107	142	40	218
Nondurable goods	828	64	154	145	73	122	82	73	18	97
Transportation and public utilities	352	14	61	83	34	34	33	41	19	32
Wholesale and retail trade	740	41	100	182	68	132	40	54	32	90
Finance and service industries	648	22	122	133	45	70	32	54	39	132
Public administration	84	2	10	22	5	13	4	8	5	16
Other industries[2]	272	5	20	40	28	38	45	49	27	19
Employment status in January 1984										
Employed	3,058	171	428	621	276	461	209	344	148	399
Unemployed	1,299	48	225	400	96	117	113	85	33	181
Percent less than 5 weeks	22.1	(3)	24.1	21.2	13.0	29.4	17.3	25.4	(3)	18.4
Percent 27 weeks or more	38.8	(3)	36.8	47.2	47.5	25.5	51.7	29.8	(3)	28.0
Not in the labor force	733	41	141	185	54	85	56	55	30	86

[1]Data refer to persons with tenure of 3 years or more who lost or left a job between January 1979 and January 1984 because of plant closings or moves, slack work, or the abolishment or their positions or shifts.

[2]Includes a small number who did not report industry.

[3]Data not shown where base is less than 75,000.

NOTE: The following list shows the States which make up each of the geographical divisions used in this table: New England—Connecticut, Maine, Massachusetts, New Hampshire, Rhode Island, and Vermont; Middle Atlantic—New Jersey, New York, and Pennsylvania; East North Central—Illinois, Indiana, Michigan, Ohio, and Wisconsin; West North Central—Iowa, Kansas, Minnesota, Missouri, Nebraska, North Dakota, and South Dakota; South Atlantic—Delaware, District of Columbia, Florida, Georgia, Maryland, North Carolina, South Carolina, Virginia, and West Virginia; East South Central—Alabama, Kentucky, Mississippi, and Tennessee; West South Central—Arkansas, Louisiana, Oklahoma, and Texas; Mountain—Arizona, Colorado, Idaho, Montana, Nevada, New Mexico, Utah, and Wyoming; Pacific—Alaska, California, Hawaii, Oregon, and Washington.

Source: Paul O. Flaim and Ellen Sehgal, "Displaced Workers of 1979-83: How Well Have They Fared?" *Monthly Labor Review*, U.S. Department of Labor, Bureau of Labor Statistics, June 1985, p 6.

placed. About 45 percent were earning as much or more in these new jobs.[21]

The BLS survey provides valuable insights into the nature of displacement, for example, the tendency toward concentration in particular industries, occupations, and geographic regions. Although displaced workers were drawn from a broad spectrum of industries and occupations, manufacturing and blue-collar workers were disproportionately represented (Figure 15). Of the 5.1 million workers considered displaced, almost one-half had lost jobs in manufacturing, a sector which now accounts for barely one-fifth of total employment. The workers most affected were those (1.7 million) in the durable goods industries, particularly steel, auto, and machinery (except electrical). Many of the displaced (1.8 million) had been employed in factory floor jobs as operators, fabricators, and laborers. In addition, a particularly large number (1.2 million) resided in the East North Central region, which includes the heavily industrialized Midwest states.

THE RANGE OF ADJUSTMENT EXPERIENCE

The survey also indicates a broad range of post-displacement experience. Figure 16, for example, shows that median weeks without work ranged from a low thirteen weeks for reemployed workers to a high of fifty-seven weeks for workers who had left the labor force. The Figure also shows that workers fifty-five years and older were

Figure 16

Displaced workers[1] by weeks without work,[2] age, and employment status, January 1984

| Characteristic | Weeks without work | | | | | |
	Less than 5 Weeks	5 to 14 Weeks	15 to 25 Weeks	27 to 52 Weeks	More than 52 Weeks	Median Weeks Without Work
Total:						
Age 20 and over	1,173	912	707	983	1,211	24.1
25 to 54 years	858	729	538	745	871	23.1
55 years and over	203	109	122	179	302	29.8
Employed:						
Age 20 and over	910	657	453	590	393	13.1
25 to 54 years	705	540	364	486	334	13.4
55 years and over	119	65	52	63	41	12.4
Unemployed:						
Age 20 and over	166	201	201	264	447	32.2
25 to 54 years	124	158	142	185	348	32.5
55 years and over	25	31	50	65	88	33.3
Not in the labor force:						
Age 20 and over	98	55	53	130	370	56.8
25 to 54 years	27	34	33	74	189	57.8
55 years and over	59	14	19	51	173	61.2

1. "Displaced" refers to persons whose jobs were lost because of plant closings or moves, slack work, or the abolishment of their positions or shifts.

2. Median period without work need not have been a continuous spell and could have included time spent outside the labor force.

Source: Paul O. Flaim and Ellen Sehgal, "Displaced Workers of 1979-83: How Well Have They Fared?" *Monthly Labor Review*, U.S. Department of Labor, Bureau of Labor Statistics, June 1985, p. 10.

Figure 17

Comparison of current to trend-adjusted former earnings, distribution of displaced workers reemployed January 1984*

	Total (%)	More than 50%	24.9 to 50%	.001 to 25%	0 & below (no loss)
			Earnings Loss		
All Reemployed					
Blue-Collar	100.0	15.5	19.2	27.7	37.6
Male	100.0	15.4	19.4	27.1	38.1
Female	100.0	15.7	18.4	30.2	35.7
White-Collar	100.0	14.2	17.6	27.5	40.7
Male	100.0	11.1	17.8	25.6	45.6
Female	100.0	17.5	17.5	29.6	35.3
Reemployed full-time					
Blue-Collar	100.0	10.1	18.6	30.2	41.1
Male	100.0	10.5	19.3	29.4	40.8
Female	100.0	8.6	15.6	33.6	42.2
White-Collar	100.0	7.4	17.0	29.9	45.7
Male	100.0	7.6	17.3	26.7	48.4
Female	100.0	7.1	16.7	34.0	42.2

*Based on larger sample of workers displaced between January 1979 and January 1983 (9.5m vs 5.1m BLS) due to elimination of 3-year tenure criterion. In this sample, the total of displaced workers reemployed in January 1984 is 6,087,000.

Source: Michael Podgursky and Paul Swaim, "Labor Market Adjustment and Job Displacement: Evidence from the January 1984 Displaced Worker Survey," Bureau of International Labor Affairs, U.S. Department of Labor, January 1986.

Figure 18

Earnings losses by weeks of joblessness, displaced workers reemployed January 1984[1]

		Percent of Earnings Loss		
Weeks of Joblessness	**Blue-Collar**		**White-Collar and Services**	
	Male	Female	Male	Female
0-14	3.9	(.7)*	(4.2)	12.4
15-26	11.7	14.3	(.6)	15.4
27-52	17.6	13.5	27.7	26.6
53+	40.4	33.2	40.3	51.8

1. Workers displaced from full-time nonagricultural jobs between 1979 and 1983 and reemployed in full-time jobs as of January 1984. Weekly earnings adjusted for trend growth; total sample of 6,087,000 workers.

*Negative loss signifies earnings gain.

Source: Michael Podgursky and Paul Swaim, "Labor Market Adjustment and Job Displacement: Evidence from the January 1984 Displaced Worker Survey," Bureau of International Labor Affairs, U.S. Department of Labor, January 1986.

out of work longer (thirty weeks) than their younger counterparts (twenty-three weeks). In addition, the range of earnings losses was particularly broad for blue-collar workers. Those displaced from mining had average losses of 34.2 percent, while displaced textile workers lost an average 2.5 percent upon reemployment. Blue-collar workers as a group, however, tended to experience greater initial earnings losses in their new jobs than did white-collar workers (Figure 17). Nearly 29 percent of blue-collar (compared to 24.4 percent of white-collar) workers had full-time weekly earnings losses of 25 percent or more. About 10 percent (compared to 7.4 percent of white-collar) had full-time losses of 50 percent or more.

According to the survey, other significant factors also influenced a worker's adjustment experience:

- Workers with the longest spells of joblessness tended to be reemployed in jobs paying considerably less than their old jobs (Figure 18).
- Higher levels of educational attainment significantly reduced the duration of joblessness and increased earnings for virtually all groups of workers.
- Local economic conditions affected the adjustment experience to the extent that each additional percentage point in the area unemployment rate added one to four weeks of joblessness and lowered reemployment earnings by 1 to 3 percent.
- More than one-half of the reemployed workers in the BLS survey were no longer in the industry group from which they have been displaced; similar movement occurred between occupations (Figures 19 and 20).
- Industry and occupational changes were especially costly for blue-collar workers (Figure 21).

Figure 19

Displaced workers by industry of lost job and industry of job held by those reemployed in January 1984

				Manufacturing			Transportation & Public Utilities	Whole-Sale and Retail Trade		
Industry of lost job	Total Displaced (Thousands)[1]	Total Reemployed	Construc-tion	Total	Durable Goods	Non-Durable Goods			Services	Other[2]
Total, 20 years and over	5,091	3,058	324	865	572	294	229	633	642	361
Construction	401	281	123	17	11	6	12	35	65	29
Manufacturing	2,483	1,474	109	693	459	234	74	227	248	124
Durable goods	1,675	980	83	452	390	62	53	163	153	76
Nondurable goods	808	493	25	240	69	171	22	63	95	48
Transportation and public utilities	336	198	23	24	15	9	84	23	23	20
Wholesale and retail trade	732	455	19	66	41	25	25	228	76	41
Services	506	347	26	42	28	14	13	67	161	38
Other[2]	633	300	26	22	15	7	19	53	71	109

1. Data refer to persons with tenure of 3 or more years who lost or left a job between January 1979 and January 1984 because of plant closings or moves, slack work, or the abolishment of their positions or shifts.

2. Includes mining; finance, insurance, and real estate; public administration; and farming, forestry, and fisheries.

Source: Paul O. Flaim and Ellen Sehgal, "Displaced Workers of 1979-83: How Well Have They Fared?" *Monthly Labor Review*, U.S. Department of Labor, Bureau of Labor Statistics, June 1985, pp. 23, 29, Tables B-5, B-11.

Figure 20

Displaced workers by occupation on job lost and occupation on job held by those reemployed in January 1984[1]

Occupation on job lost	Total Displaced[2]	Total Reemployed	Occupation on job held on January 1984					
			Managerial and Professional Specialty	Technical, Sales and Administrative Support	Service Occupations	Precision Production, Craft, and Repair	Operators, Fabricators, and Laborers	Farming Forestry, and Fishing
Total, 20 years and over[3]	5,091	3,058	476	796	320	621	793	52
Managerial and Professional specialty	703	525	269	157	31	38	28	2
Technical, sales, and Administrative support	1,162	704	108	426	56	50	62	3
Service occupations	275	140	7	20	81	18	14	--
Precision production, craft, and repair	1,042	642	52	57	35	359	131	9
Operators, fabricators, and laborers	1,823	995	32	132	118	145	543	26
Farming, forestry, and fishing	68	47	5	3	0	9	17	13

1. Thousands

2. Data refer to persons with tenure of 3 or more years who lost or left a job between January 1979 and January 1984 because of plant closings or moves, slack work, or the abolishment of their positions or shifts.

3. Total includes a small number who did not report occupation.

Source: Paul O. Flaim and Ellen Sehgal, "Displaced Workers of 1979-83: How Well Have They Fared?" *Monthly Labor Review*, U.S. Department of Labor, Bureau of Labor Statistics, June 1985, pp. 5, 13, Tables 3, 12.

Figure 21

Average earnings losses by change of industry or occupation, displaced workers with five or more years of tenure reemployed January 1984[1]

	Percent of Earnings Loss	
	New Industry	New Occupation
Blue-Collar	28.3	26.0
Male	28.7	26.1
Female	24.0	24.5
White-Collar	18.3	16.4
Male	26.2	11.5
Female	14.1	25.2

1. Workers displaced from full-time nonagricultural and salary jobs with 5+ years tenure between January 1979 and January 1983, and reemployed full-time in a new industry or occupation as of January 1984; weekly earnings adjusted for trend growth.

Source: Michael Podgursky and Paul Swaim, "Labor Market Adjustment and Job Displacement: Evidence from the January 1984 Displaced Worker Survey," Bureau of International Labor Affairs, U.S. Department of Labor, January 1986.

These findings underscore the point that the issue of displacement is really the issue of adjustment, especially concerning the quality of labor market experience following the permanent loss of a job. **To be effective, policy responses will need to distinguish between different adjustment experiences. For the majority of displaced workers, the present system of broad-based income support may be sufficient. More targeted approaches may be needed, however, for workers requiring new skills or further education.**

Finally, we need to know more about the displaced worker. Most of what we know to date is based on measurements taken between 1979 and 1984, an unusually difficult period that began with double-digit inflation and included two recessions, an average unemployment rate of 8 percent, and a 50 percent increase in the foreign exchange value of the dollar. Much more needs to be known about the experience and quality of adjustment over time to understand the changing needs of people and the ways in which opportunities can be expanded and hardships lessened.

Perhaps most important of all, the structural shift in occupations suggests that the distinction between manufacturing and services is becoming less important than what people actually do and whether they have the education and skills to help them move up the earnings ladder.

CHAPTER III:
ADJUSTMENT POLICIES IN THE PRIVATE SECTOR

The present debate over adjustment policies suffers from too much narrow vision and bad timing. Policy makers too often focus on what to do in specific events like plant closings which take place only after a business fails. By so doing, they are missing the larger competitive context which helps determine the success or failure of an enterprise. Consequently, policies in both the public and private sectors too often are formulated defensively, addressing only partially the actual challenges facing both businesses and workers.

Effective adjustment cannot be achieved if it is attempted as a last-minute effort by management to prepare workers for the competitive failure of a business, or as a last-minute effort by labor leaders to forestall a plant closing. Companies need to be responsive on a regular basis to a variety of situations involving actual or potential displacement, including that which occurs as a result of actions taken to ensure competitive success. This may sound easy enough, but in reality it will often require radical changes in the ways that management and workers, union and nonunion, relate to each other and to the enterprise.

In this chapter we cite a number of examples of efforts companies are making to meet the dual challenges of increased competitiveness and adjustment.

THE PRODUCTIVITY IMPERATIVE

Several of CED's previous policy statements have emphasized the importance of improving productivity. America's businesses need to produce more, at less cost, and with superior quality to compete successfully in today's markets. The challenge is great, particularly given the fact that since 1960 the rate of productivity growth in the United States has fallen considerably behind that of our major competitors. Manufacturing productivity growth rates in most industrialized countries exceeded that of the United States during the 1960s and 1970s. As a result, these countries gained rapidly on the level of U.S. productivity. In Japan, for example, productivity in this sector increased about three times as fast as ours during this period. By 1981, Japanese manufacturing productivity matched our own (Figure 22).

Increased productivity has been the key to economic progress, bringing with it gains in real income and improved ability to compete. Nations that have suffered prolonged slowdowns in productivity have inevitably forfeited their economic preeminence. The same holds true for industries that have been unable to adopt, or have resisted adopting, productivity improvements and as a result have been overcome by more efficient, higher quality producers. The failure of the United States to make substantial improvements in productivity over the last decade has been a major

Figure 22

Convergence of U.S. and Japanese Manufacturing Productivity Levels

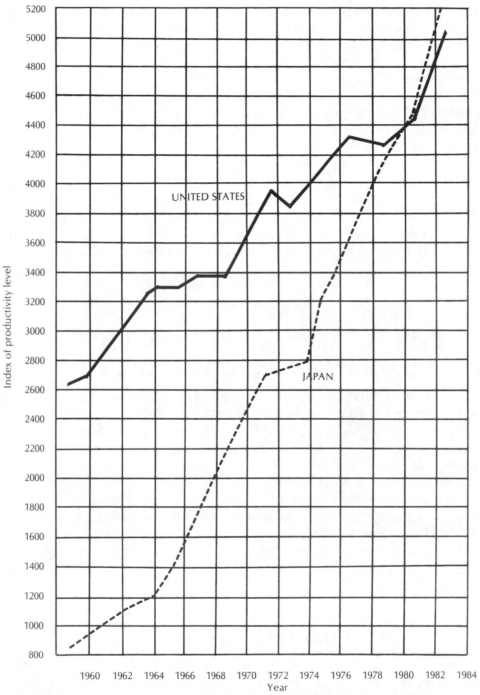

The benchmark year for the comparative levels is 1977. The relative productivity levels for 1977 are based on the Japan Productivity Center's industry comparison of most manufacturing industries in each country for the 1970s. These results, including productivity growth rates, were similar to available data from the U.S. Bureau of Labor Statistics. To determine the estimates for the period 1960 to 1981, the U.S. government's growth rate statistics were applied to the Japan Productivity Center's 1977 productivity level estimates.

cause of our current competitive problems. It has also increased our vulnerability to unfavorable shifts in the value of the dollar.[1]

While few would dispute the important positive relationship between productivity and competitiveness, there is much less agreement and greater concern over the effects of productivity on employment. From the vantage point of the plant floor, it often seems that greater productivity means fewer jobs, especially when labor-saving technology and other process changes are made to reduce per unit labor costs.

The fact is that productivity gains may be accompanied by increases or decreases in employment. Market demand is obviously a critical factor in determining how many jobs are affected. Productivity improvements introduced in businesses enjoying growing markets are more likely to result in new jobs being created, especially when the business manages to achieve cost leadership. On the other hand, productivity-enhancing measures taken when markets are declining or simply not growing usually involve some loss of jobs. Firms handle this in different ways. IBM, for example, used voluntary separations and redeployment of workers to increase productivity and regain market share. (See box on page 27.)

The productivity imperative, however, applies whether markets are growing or declining. In either case, businesses cannot afford to risk losing market share to more efficient producers, especially foreign producers that have already achieved economies of scale in their home markets. Productivity gains are the most important means for improving cost position and anticipating changes in demand or the entry of new rivals capable of shifting the balance of competitive advantage.

THE WORKER'S STAKE IN THE COMPANY'S PERFORMANCE

The productivity imperative requires companies to reallocate resources quickly in response to present or anticipated changes in the marketplace. New technology and product processes will have to be applied. In other cases, plants that are either outmoded or creating excess capacity will have to be closed.

But capital investments and plant rationalizations are not the only or necessarily the most important means of achieving productivity gains. The commitment of people to the success of the enterprise is critical. Unfortunately, the communication and compensation systems in many companies still follow a hierarchical approach that stresses the divergence between employers and employees. Effective networks for information-sharing frequently do not exist. In addition, prevailing wage systems encourage employees to perceive their pay and benefit increases as being independent of the company's level of productivity or profitability.

COMMUNICATION

The uncertainties and anxieties created by change increase the need for effective communication among all levels of the organization, as well as with key individuals and groups in the plant community.

First and foremost, employees need to know about the competitive realities, both good and bad, confronting the business. They also need to know what actions are necessary to strengthen the business and the rewards they can expect to receive for contributing to the business's success. Companies should view the communication of these important messages as an opportunity to rally support and, in the event of a plant closing or other action involving employment loss, as an opportunity to facilitate the move to a new job.

> ## REDEPLOYING WORKERS FOR IMPROVED PRODUCTIVITY: THE IBM BURLINGTON PLANT
>
> In 1982, IBM was faced with a significantly reduced demand for the semi-conductor memory chips produced at its Burlington, Vermont, facility. A combination of aggressive Japanese pricing, the 1981-82 recession, and the company's practice of allowing other IBM production units to purchase the lowest cost component, whatever the source, forced the Burlington plant management to make rapid improvements in its productivity.
>
> The plant adopted a wide number of human resource policies designed to redeploy workers, through either voluntary separation (via retirement, a special early retirement incentive, and approved transfers to other plants) or by encouraging employees to shift from indirect jobs to direct production work. This latter effort required particular care and relied in large measure on the long-standing good will and open communication between management and employees.
>
> The effect of these efforts was to reduce the indirect, non-production part of the work force by 488 workers without causing large-scale layoffs or involuntary separations. The Burlington plant today is the biggest facility of its kind in the world.

Two-way communication that is open, candid, and done on a regular basis builds credibility and trust.

Elements of an effective communication strategy include:

- Commitment by top business management to communicate business goals, plans, issues, and challenges.
- A company-wide training effort for effective management/employee communications.
- Ongoing communication regarding basic facts:
  - markets, customers, costs, earnings, investment, productivity, and quality which determine the business's success;
  - the job package of pay, benefits, and protection which all employees receive in return for their contributions to the business.
- Targeted communication programs focusing on specific business and compensation issues.
- The use of spokespeople drawn from both management and labor, and a variety of media to communicate key messages.

An example of successful communication took place during the revamping of GE's dishwasher operations in Louisville, Kentucky, where early communication was key to effecting change. (See box on page 28.)

Another example involves the memorandum of mutual agreement which Pacific Bell and Nevada Bell signed with the Communications Workers of America to provide employment security while adapting to change. (See box on page 28.)

FLEXIBLE TOTAL COMPENSATION

Open communication of business realities is one way to promote the sense of common purpose or personal stake in the success of the enterprise. Another is to

---

AUTOMATION AND COMMUNICATION

In a move designed to keep its Major Appliance business vital and competitive, GE launched a plan for the 1980s to invest a billion dollars in its core product lines. The program focused on quality control and automation to meet the strong challenges of competition in the marketplace. The company's dishwasher assembly operations in Louisville, Kentucky, was selected to receive the first $60 million.

Early communication with employees about the need for change was regarded as a priority. Employees, management, and union leaders met to discuss the realities of the marketplace. Worker involvement programs put to use the wealth of knowledge on the factory floor. Teams of workers were sent to suppliers' factories to participate in the design phase, and workers implemented improvement in production operations.

Increases in production and productivity boosted GE's share of the dishwasher market by 10 points in two and a half years. Although employment reductions were forecast, automation of the dishwasher line cost no jobs because of the industry's recovery and GE's increased market share.

---

increase the flexibility of current compensation by linking some portion of wages and benefits to company performance.* Compensation would then increase or decrease, depending on whether or not the business achieved gains in cost savings, productivity, and/or profitability.

Under fixed compensation systems employees are encouraged to view wage and benefit increases independently of business performance. Fixed compensation was a

---

EMPLOYMENT SECURITY: PRINCIPLES AND ACTIONS

In August of 1986, Pacific Bell and Nevada Bell signed contracts with the Communications Workers of America (CWA) which recognized the dramatic effects that increasing competition and new technology were having on their business. In addition, the contract recognized the profound changes that new technology has had on the business as a whole and on the skills required of communications workers.

Under the terms of the contract, Pacific Bell/Nevada Bell offers employment security through reassignment and retraining to all who meet performance standards, even if their present jobs are eliminated. This policy will continue so long as the company is successfully meeting the goals of its business plan.

The specific performance standards include utilizing personnel and/or career development designed to enable employees to adjust to technology and business changes, and the willingness of employees to accept new work assignments and new locations.

The Pacific Bell/Nevada Bell contract with the CWA importantly recognizes the effect of rapidly increasing international competition and new technology on business and on the nature of people's jobs in the many changing areas of the telecommunications industry.

---

*See memorandum by SIDNEY J. WEINBERG, JR. (page 53.)

stabilizing influence on workers' income as long as markets were growing and competition was limited to domestic producers. Under present conditions, fixed compensation is actually a destabilizing influence because it fails to prepare workers for the type of rapid, structural changes that are occurring and that directly affect employment.[2]

Changes, however, have already begun to take place in the wage-setting policies of American companies. A Conference Board survey of major companies in late 1983 found that a growing number were responding to competitive pressures by basing wage changes on internal criteria, such as labor cost per unit of output, or expected profits. This shift signals a dramatic change from policies prevalent during the 1970s which were based on imitation of other companies' wage increases and which produced an inflexible system unresponsive to business conditions.[3]

FLEXIBLE COMPENSATION: THE NUCOR EXAMPLE

In an industry hard-hit by competition from imports, the specialty steel company Nucor relies on the most advanced technology available and a sophisticated human relations system to remain successful.

The centerpiece of the human relations system is a flexible compensation package which ties work performance and productivity to each employee's compensation, from the work crew to top management. Nucor employees are paid a lower-than-average base salary, with a built-in bonus incentive system which can increase the base pay by as much as 50 to 60 percent according to the performance of an employee's work team. The compensation levels therefore vary with the competitive success of the business on a weekly basis, offering employees a stake in the success of the business, and cushioning the company against the cyclical swings of the steel industry.

Nucor's productivity levels now rival those of its international competitors, and Nucor employees continue to earn higher annual pay than their counterparts in other steel companies. The flexible compensation system enables Nucor to hold onto its employees during slowdowns, and the company has maintained a no layoff policy for over fourteen years.

For example, from 1973 to 1981, hourly compensation rose about as much in industries with declining productivity as in industries with productivity growth. In many manufacturing industries, prices rose strongly while productivity declined or increased slowly. Thus, beginning in 1973, prices and unit labor costs in manufacturing accelerated, as hourly compensation increased and productivity growth slowed down. Such a situation was tolerable only as long as companies were able to continue raising prices as a means of recouping higher labor costs. The tolerance came to an abrupt end in the early 1980s as inflation dropped and the strong dollar further increased the disadvantage of American firms.[4]

The shift from imitation and formula patterning to internal criteria of wage setting and company bargaining is a positive development. Unfortunately, since it is still associated with "concessions" won by management during the recession years of 1981 to 1982, "flexible total compensation" is often misunderstood as being a euphemism for lower wages, lower benefits, or a smaller share of economic growth for employees. That is clearly not the case. The flexibility stems from the fact that compensation can go up as well as down.

The Nucor Company provides an example of a successful flexible compensation plan in an industry with a traditionally inflexible wage pattern. (See page 29.)

Most current flexible plans keep a fixed base of wages or salary and add to that a general or group incentive, usually in the form of a bonus linked to increases in productivity, profitability, or some combination of cost savings. Formulas vary from plan to plan, depending on the criteria used. For example, units of output can be used to measure productivity, or return on sales can be used in calculating profitability. Bonuses also vary.

In the Scanlon Plan, for instance, productivity or "gain-sharing" bonuses are based on a plant's total payroll cost compared with the sales value of production. A bonus is paid when the actual payroll cost as a percent of sales value is less than the standard payroll cost. The savings are shared between the company and employees on a 25/75 percentage basis. An integral part of the plan is the establishment of production screening committees to review and approve or reject suggestions for productivity improvement measures.[5]

The introduction of reward systems based on flexible compensation may in some cases require the dismantling of company-wide compensation systems that are no longer responsive to the needs of the business or employees. As competition increases and new rivals cause the restructuring of industries, both companies and their employees are going to feel the need to respond to variable business conditions. Tailored reward systems such as gainsharing are one response. Another response is to broaden the array of trade-offs available to employers and employees, particularly those trade-offs which better reflect the competitive conditions of the enterprise and the makeup of its work force.

Old-line manufacturing firms in mature industries with a relatively high-wage, long-tenured work force could then offer to alter the mix of compensation by providing smaller wage gains in return for increased displacement rights and income protection benefits. The company trades off increased costs in the event of business failure for increased ability to control wage growth and improve its position against lower-cost competitors. Workers sacrifice current income for greater future protection and security or a share in the rewards of a return to financial health, through a profit-sharing or stock ownership arrangement. In some mature industries where the tradition of patterned settlements is well established, moving to more flexible systems may require intermediary steps.

Firms in mature industries are not the only ones that could benefit from a broadening of trade-off opportunities. A start-up or venture business with a relatively low-wage, short-tenured work force in a risk-oriented environment could alter the mix of compensation to emphasize immediate wage gains as a trade-off for lower retention benefits via pensions or other forms of income security. Or firms in high-technology-product industries with a high-wage, mobile work force could trade off increased levels of single-employer pension accumulation benefits for lower levels of benefits with greater portability.

In general, total flexible compensation is better suited to current competitive realities than mandated, monolithic pay and benefit practices because it encourages organizational innovation and creative responses to difficult business conditions.

THE IMPORTANCE OF MOBILITY

Americans are usually willing to take the risks involved in reaching for new opportunity in order to improve their current situation or build toward a better future for their children. **Higher rates of mobility for both capital and labor permit the more efficient reallocation of resources and, thus, give the United States a competitive advantage over other countries.**[6]

Although U.S. workers still have the edge, there has been some falloff in geographic mobility in recent years. The percentage of the population moving each year has declined. So has the percentage of unemployed who quit their jobs. Both economic and demographic reasons have been offered to help explain this change. For example, the huge rise in the number of two-income families, and the high cost of housing make moving more difficult.[7] Age is another factor. The BLS survey on displaced workers found that only 6 percent of workers aged fifty-five and over, compared to fifteen percent of workers aged twenty-five to thirty-four, moved to a different city or county to look for work or take a different job. Of those who did move, however, a higher proportion became reemployed.[8]

In addition to geographic mobility, occupational and industrial mobility are increasingly important factors in adapting to change. The same BLS survey found that about half of the displaced workers who subsequently became reemployed were in occupations and industries different from those of their lost jobs.[9]

The structural changes occurring in markets clearly put a premium on the ability of workers to move easily and quickly to new opportunity. That movement can take place not only between, but also within industries and firms. Companies are experiencing the same occupational shifts evident in the larger economy. Roughly half of the 1 million new jobs created in manufacturing firms between 1969 and 1979 were in typically white-collar technical and professional occupations.[10]

Companies can help prepare employees for changes in employment in at least three ways: (1) providing training for new skills; (2) giving advance notice of business decisions affecting jobs; and (3) redesigning benefit plans to help ease the transition to new work.

EDUCATION AND TRAINING

Companies spend an estimated $30 to $50 billion a year formally educating and training employees. Informal training has been estimated to run as high as $180 billion a year.[11] This activity has continued to grow in recent years as a result of the rapid introduction of new technology and the adoption of new corporate strategies and goals to respond to changes in the business environment. Senior managers are expected to have enough of a grasp of the technologies underlying new products and processes to make critical investment decisions. Production workers are expected to acquire new skills to match the work that needs to be done.

Heightened global competition also requires new skills and knowledge, as well as attitudinal changes, particularly in industries unused to thinking in terms of world markets. An increasing number of companies, for example, are beginning to view changing competition as the primary factor changing the structure of their industries. As a result, business managers are being armed with the latest in competitive analysis and strategy to fend off the challenges presented by the entry of new rivals into their markets. The first objective of company training is to prepare both management and their employees for change by developing skills that lead to improved productivity, performance, and profitability and support the corporation's strategic objectives. Such training should be measured by its effect on the business and on improving the return on investment.

In-house retraining can also qualify individuals who become displaced from a current job for new opportunities within the company or outside. **First and foremost, companies should make every effort to retrain their existing work force for the new jobs being created in their businesses.** Northern Telecom's Data Systems Division provides one such example of dramatic improvements in production made possible in part by the retraining of its operating and staff personnel. (See below.) In many cases, skills are transferable and reassignment to another job requires little or no retraining. However, in other cases such as Northern Telecom's, higher skills are a prerequisite. Indeed, most in-house training is undertaken to prepare employees for opportunities within the company. The direct link to a new job provides a powerful incentive to acquire new skills and is the chief reason why such training is so successful.

In addition, company training programs should enable displaced workers to qualify for employment outside of the firm. This can be done either in-house or through education and training allowances or tuition-refund payments.

The Ford Motor Company provides in-depth career counseling and job development, including tuition assistance. Ford considers this a comprehensive service geared toward lifetime education for auto workers. (See page 33.)

Accepting the responsibility to prepare workers for outside jobs will require a radical change in the way most companies view their investment strategy in human resources. Employers traditionally have been reluctant to invest in training unless it was tied directly to jobs within the firm. Preparing a work force for some other company's benefit has never had much appeal.

Yet company training programs need to take into account the fact that in many industries employment security may rest more on the development of transferable

---

RETRAINING FOR HIGHER-SKILLED WORK

Faced with the challenge to make substantial improvements both in production and quality level, Northern Telecom's Data Systems Division in Minneapolis decided to invest in worker retraining and make dramatic changes in management technique and production process.

The training started with senior management and progressed to all employees within the manufacturing operation. The new system was designed to run with small, closely knit teams of operators, integrating quality control into the new production process. Almost 600 members of the production teams were trained in the program basics and statistical techniques. In addition, 150 staff members were trained in problem solving and group dynamics.

The end result was a reduction in the start-to-finish assembly time from seven and a half days to eighty-eight minutes. The labor component of assembly was reduced by 40 percent, and the amount of floor space required dropped by 70 percent. Morale was also enhanced because the employees recognized their selection for retraining as a vote of confidence in them by the company. Northern Telecom's retraining effort was therefore successful, not only in enhancing the company's competitive position in the marketplace, but also in increasing the dedication and motivation of its work force.

PREPARING EMPLOYEES FOR FUTURE EMPLOYMENT

The auto industry, faced with long-term declines in productivity and severe competition in both foreign and domestic markets, had to include comprehensive labor policies in its strategy to adjust to changes in the marketplace. The Ford Motor Company and United Auto Workers (UAW) Joint Employee Development and Training Program articulated a set of principles and established Career Services and Reemployment Assistance Centers in order to meet this challenge.

The Assistance Centers offer a carefully ordered and comprehensive set of services for Ford employees facing layoffs or job changes. Participants receive personal development services including individualized needs assessment and support services for the worker and family when necessary. Career counseling is offered, as well as basic skills training and prepaid tuition assistance at all academic levels. In the Training and Placement Component, the participant can be referred to vocational retraining classes, or on-the-job-training. Job development resources are offered, including sessions in job-search skills and placement services.

The Ford/UAW Centers demonstrate that comprehensive, individualized services can be offered with a long-range view toward lifetime education and career development for the workers.

skills than on long-term service in one company. Training programs and new work patterns emphasizing work-share, teamwork, and "pay for knowledge" broaden employees' skills and enhance their mobility both within and outside the firm. At its Livonia engine plant, General Motors has established a pay for knowledge program

TEAM WORK AND PAY FOR KNOWLEDGE

When General Motors' Cadillac Motor Car Division moved its Detroit engine works plant to the nearby community of Livonia, the company introduced a new work system built on a concept of team building and employee participation in decision making.

The plant work force, which included 95 percent of the workers from the former site, was divided into fifteen departments and then divided further into work teams of ten to twenty employees. Presently, within their teams, the employees rotate jobs, fill in for absent employees, and explore ways to redesign the work flow for greater productivity. Employees are paid on the basis of the new skills they acquire through a "pay-for-knowledge" system that provides incentives for employees to develop new skills and increase their flexibility at performing a variety of tasks.

The new work system was a significant factor in allowing the Livonia plant to hit the break-even point a full year sooner than anticipated. The plant uses less manpower per engine while increasing product quality. In addition, employees have found that the team system offers them greater opportunities for skills development and decision making within the plant.

which provides incentives to encourage employees to learn new skills. (See page 33.)

The fact of displacement, in short, requires companies to examine a broader array of trade-offs to ensure freedom and flexibility in making difficult but necessary business decisions. As education in general is strongly correlated with ease of adjustment, company investments in training and education can play a key role in ensuring that workers faced with displacement will be able to move to new opportunity.

ADVANCE NOTICE

Companies should provide as much notice as possible of decisions affecting jobs, particularly in cases of plant closings, work transfers, or automation. Advance notice allows employees time to adjust and allows management time to plan and implement business moves in such a way as to minimize hardship. Companies should also take steps to notify the local community and state agencies of pending plant-closings in order to allow time for a coordinated response. A recent Conference Board survey of company plant-closing practices found that the longer the notice given, the more likely that support programs, such as retraining and outplacement, were offered.[12]

Some companies are reluctant to provide notice, fearful of employee disruptions and a falloff in productivity. Experience, however, suggests the contrary. Company managers responding to the Conference Board survey believed that advance notice, combined with generous severance payments, reduces pressure and anxiety, generates good will, and contributes to improved productivity.[13]

Advance notice is most effective when combined with other support programs. The time given should be used to help prepare workers for new opportunity. Job counseling and job-search workshops are especially useful when they provide information about job openings in the community and in neighboring areas. The Business Roundtable and other employer groups have established voluntary guidelines on plant closings and have urged companies to implement the most practical combination of policies to help workers affected by these changes.[14] (See page 35.)

Since the competitive situation and financial resources of companies vary, the amount of notice and program support should be determined by individual firms. Statutorily requiring companies to give a fixed period of notice in cases of plant closings, for example, would make little sense for firms that suffer the sudden loss of major contracts and, as a result, find themselves out of business overnight. In addition, the small and medium-size venture companies that are major job generators tend to operate in high-risk business environments. Flexibility is critical to their success; the costs of failure have to be kept low or the incentive to start up again will be lost.

Mandatory notice would, therefore, have the effect of inhibiting job generation and delaying the very adjustment process which is vital to our competitiveness. It would also increase labor market rigidities at the very time that other countries, many of which are experiencing high unemployment, are seeking to emulate the flexibility of the U.S. system.

Mandatory notice would also have the effect of making the issue of adjustment that of notice alone. More important than the symbolic value of requiring a fixed period of notice is the provision of benefits and other support programs that can affect the quality of adjustment. The composition of this package should be worked out between employers and employees. In the presence of a union, collective bargaining should provide the context in which trade-offs can be made, taking into consideration the economic and financial conditions of the business.

REORIENTING BENEFIT PROGRAMS

Perhaps the most radical rethinking needs to be done in the area of employee benefits. Most benefit programs currently are oriented to career-long employment with the same firm and thus discourage mobility outside the firm. Displaced workers, therefore, suffer an incredible loss of short- and long-term benefits, particularly if they

---

BUSINESS ROUNDTABLE PLANT CLOSING GUIDELINES

1. NOTICE -- Provide the longest practicable notification to affected workers and communities.
2. COMMUNICATION -- Devise and conduct a communication program that is coordinated with the employees and the affected public bodies, such as state and local government leaders.
3. SEVERANCE PAY -- Devise and provide a program of severance assistance based on factors such as length of service, compensation level, level of prior responsibilities, and outside payments.
4. BENEFIT EXTENSION -- Assure responsible continuation of appropriate benefits.
5. PENSION -- Special consideration might be given in company policies, programs, and/or in collective bargaining agreements to such issues as liberalized retirement plan provisions, benefit eligibility, or extending pension credits during severance periods.
6. OUTPLACEMENT -- The firm may operate independently or in conjunction with state and federal agencies' outplacement assistance. Such assistance could include counseling of workers, job fairs, and the identification of potential job vacancies.
7. RETRAINING -- The form may assist the worker secure retraining either through public programs or company operated programs.
8. COMMUNITY RELATIONS -- The firm may work with the community to redeploy the closed plant. Such efforts could include assistance in creating and operating a local economic development program; informing state and private economic development agencies of the potential uses and availability of the facilities; or sale of the business.

These recommendations are a compilation of the various elements of programs in industry today. Such recommendations should be designed to assist people in reestablishing themselves in our economic society.

These recommendations are severable. Each should be given consideration on its own merits and utilized as circumstances warrant.

Plant Closings Sub-Committee
June 1983

lack tenure in the firm. **Since some displacement is an inevitable result of structural changes, fundamental reexamination of issues like pension portability, medical insurance continuation, training and education benefits, severance pay options, and a variety of other benefits issues may be in order.***

Such reexamination should not signal a lessened commitment by companies to their long-tenured work force. On the contrary, companies have a special responsibility to those workers who have given long years of service, particularly since displacement usually involves greater hardship for older, longer tenured, higher paid employees. Whenever possible, adjustment for such workers should be made easier by providing larger severance payments and longer periods of uninterrupted health and life insurance coverage. Disincentives to early retirement should also be eliminated, allowing long-service workers to retire with their vested pension benefits unreduced.

However, since displacement is not confined to either long-time or even older employees, companies should shape overall benefit programs with the changing needs of their work force in mind. Benefits oriented to career-long attachment may be less desirable than those that increase mobility or at least do not penalize the move to new opportunity elsewhere.

Shorter tenured workers, for example, could have their pension-vesting periods reduced in the event of a plant closing or other permanent job loss. In addition, trade-offs could be considered, for example, between increased portability, either via shorter vesting or the establishment of defined contribution plans, and a decreased absolute level of pension payment. Right now, relatively few workers receive a high level of private pension payment while the majority receive very little or none at all. Shorter vesting periods combined with decreased absolute levels of pension payments would spread benefits among a larger number of workers as well as reduce a significant penalty for short service employment.

Similar rethinking should be done with regard to other benefits, such as savings programs and the extension of insurance coverage. Incentives to encourage increased saving should be considered, as well as payout options in the event of job termination so that employees have ready access to cash and/or securities accumulated. Whenever possible, health and life insurance coverage should be extended for a certain period of time, depending on the permanence of the job loss and on the financial health of the company. Where extension of coverage at former levels is not possible, companies should attempt to offer coverage at reduced rates.

Benefit practices are an important part of competitive strategy, because they help to shape the expectations of workers regarding the quality and security of their present and future employment. The challenge now is to reorient our thinking about the design of benefit plans so that, rather than being penalized, people are encouraged to make that next move with greater confidence.

---

*See memorandum by WILLIAM C. GREENOUGH (page 53.)

CHAPTER IV:
PUBLIC POLICIES

Change is occurring not only among individuals, firms, and markets, but also in the role of government. Not too long ago massive public spending was considered an antidote to social problems. That is no longer the case, both because of the disillusionment brought on by ineffective programs, and because of the resource limitations imposed by huge federal budget deficits. The new reality confronting government is not unlike that confronting business. Competition for markets in the private sector is being matched by an equally intense competition in the public sector for new ideas and new policies that will serve to redefine the role of government in the economy. The danger is that old approaches will simply be given new labels and the chance to restructure policies to meet changing needs will be lost.

To prevent this from happening, policy makers will have to take a broader view of structural economic change that is focused, first, on the conditions that create opportunity and, second, on the ways in which public policy can be used to ease the adjustment of displaced workers and their communities.

It is not simply a case of government picking up where the private sector leaves off. Structural economic change has created areas of responsibility that are distinctly public in nature. Only government, for example, can institute economy-wide incentives for growth, or negotiate multilateral cooperation on exchange rates or market access. And government often is in a better position to mitigate the severe hardships that result from the mismatches that can occur between opportunity and need.

THE IMPORTANCE OF
MACROECONOMIC POLICIES

All of our best efforts at adjustment will fail unless the conditions for economic growth are created. The choice of fiscal and monetary policies is critical because it helps determine the balance between gains and losses brought on by structural change.

Much of the accelerated decline in manufacturing over the past five years has resulted from the damage inflicted on U.S. exports by an uncompetitive dollar (Figure 23). The dollar's strength, regarded by some as a positive sign of other countries' confidence in the U.S. economy, in fact stemmed from our inability to control fiscal policy. Multilateral action has been taken recently to bring the dollar's value into greater alignment with other exchange rates. However, huge federal budget deficits remain a serious threat to sustained, noninflationary economic growth and a drain on the living standards of future generations.

Figure 23

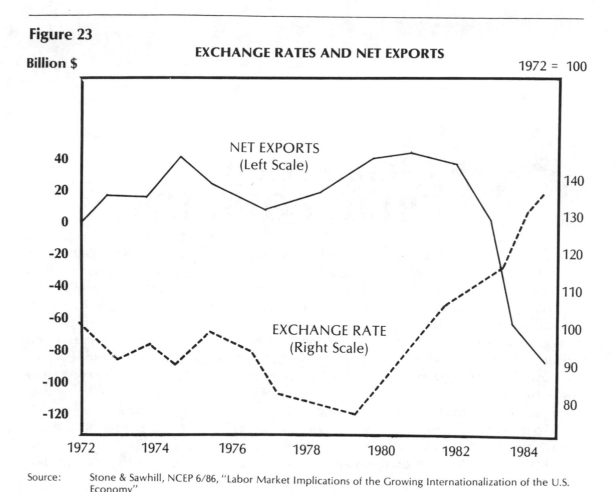

EXCHANGE RATES AND NET EXPORTS

Billion $

1972 = 100

NET EXPORTS (Left Scale)

EXCHANGE RATE (Right Scale)

Source: Stone & Sawhill, NCEP 6/86, "Labor Market Implications of the Growing Internationalization of the U.S. Economy"

For this reason, CED has continued to emphasize the importance of budget deficit reduction. Spending restraint must be exercised in all program areas, including defense, Social Security, and other major entitlements. If deficit reduction targets cannot be met solely through cuts in spending, then tax increases will have to be considered.[1]

Macroeconomic policies, however, affect more than the conditions for growth in the United States. With the increasing internationalization of markets, policies once viewed primarily in domestic terms have taken on the added significance of helping to position American companies vis-a-vis their foreign competition. Cross-country comparisons of economic and industrial performance are now indicators of competitive health. Thus, productivity improvements, even if historically high by U.S. standards, mean little if the rate of increase in other countries is two to three times as great.

Since capital investment sets the stage for rising productivity, CED has urged that tax policy serve to encourage, and not penalize, productive investment in new plant and equipment and in new technology. Historically, the U.S. cost of capital has been several times as high as that of the Japanese (Figure 24). This capital cost gap reflects a variety of factors, e.g., Japan's high savings, financial structure, and taxation. In the United States, the high cost of capital retards investment and, therefore, productivity growth relative to Japan. One of the ways it does this is by discouraging investments that do not pay off quickly. When the cost of capital is twice as high, the investment payback period can only be half as long. This is an important reason why American businessmen have shorter time horizons compared with the seemingly more patient Japanese.[2]

REORIENTING
EMPLOYMENT SECURITY PROGRAMS

When conditions for growth and competitive advantage are in place, the likelihood is greater that employment opportunities will be created in sufficient number and quality to outweigh losses. Even so, hardships will never be eliminated. Displaced workers tend to be jobless for longer periods of time than regular unemployed workers and, therefore, tend to suffer greater disruption in their personal and family lives. Furthermore, those workers in greatest need are least likely to be able to take advantage of new opportunity, either because of their age, geographic location, or skills, all of which serve to increase their attachment to a job that has ceased to exist.

Some of the hardship suffered as well as the mismatch between need and

Figure 24

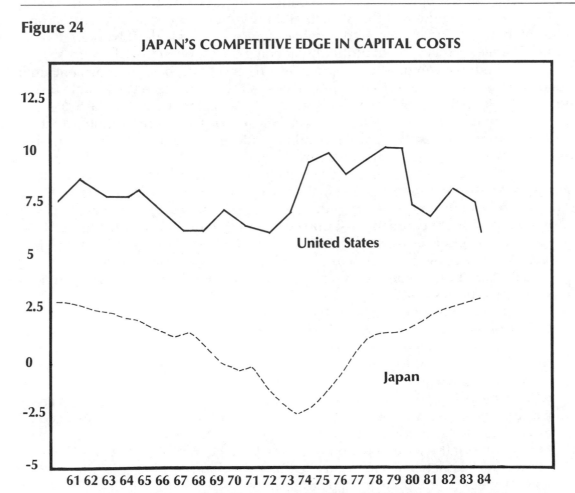

JAPAN'S COMPETITIVE EDGE IN CAPITAL COSTS

Source: George N. Hatsopoulos and Steven H. Brooks, "The Gap in the Cost of Capital: Causes, Effects, and Remedies," *Technology and Economic Policy*, eds., Ralph Landau and Dale Jorgenson, Eds. 1986.

opportunity can be ameliorated by providing support services such as counseling, job search, and retraining, and perhaps even incentives to reemployment. Amidst the mostly tentative findings about displacement, one conclusion stands out in remarkable clarity: the longer the period of joblessness, the greater the earnings loss in a new job.

Any measures that serve to encourage reemployment should, therefore, lessen hardship, especially since workers with long spells of joblessness also face a higher risk of benefits loss, such as regular and supplemental unemployment and group health insurance.

Unfortunately, Unemployment Insurance (UI), which is the public program relied on most heavily by displaced workers, is focused mostly on short-term income maintenance, by and large ignoring the fact that worker displacement involves not only permanent job loss, but often reemployment in different industries and occupations.

LAYING THE GROUNDWORK FOR REFORM

The federal-state Unemployment Insurance system is the nation's largest social program designed to assist unemployed workers. The system was originally designed to provide income maintenance for workers temporarily laid-off and expecting to be rehired by their former employer. Although states are now encouraged to provide training and other support services, UI continues to focus on simple income maintenance, overlooking the fact that structural shifts in the economy have created new adjustment needs for an increased number of permanently laid-off workers.

CED believes that ways of further broadening the scope of the UI system should be considered to overcome the disincentive to accepting new employment until benefits are exhausted and to encourage more states to increase the flexible use of benefits for training and job-search assistance. Redesigning the use of the $20 to $25 billion in annual UI expenditures presents an extraordinary opportunity to target assistance to permanently displaced workers without sacrificing the indispensable role UI plays as a source of income between jobs.

However, before any changes can be made to increase the resources available to aid displaced workers, inefficiencies in the current system need to be reduced. Many states are reluctant to experiment with new types of services, fearing that increased costs will aggravate the already weak financial position of their UI trust funds. One way to overcome this powerful inhibition to change is to discourage inappropriate application or overuse of the system by employees and employers alike.

CED, therefore, recommends that the following reforms be considered to improve the efficiency of the UI system:[3]

- **Establish minimum waiting periods, or increase those which are already required, before unemployed workers are eligible for receipt of benefits.** Inappropriate use of the UI system by workers who either fail to meet work test requirements or are on voluntary unemployment would be discouraged if the eleven states which now have no waiting period for benefits required one. In the remaining states where the waiting period is usually one week, consideration might be given to extending the period somewhat. Resources saved in this way could be used to assist the long-term unemployed.

  For example, if the waiting period were ten days, the traditional twenty-six weeks of regular UI benefits would begin after this period and continue past the twenty-seventh week of unemployment. The initial cost of days without UI benefits would be borne by all workers and would be one way of introducing the concept of coinsurance into the current system.

- **Strengthen the relationship between the firms's unemployment experience and the UI tax that it pays.** All states have some form of experience rating in which the employer tax is related to the amount of unemployment an employer has generated in the past. However, the proportion of benefits subject to the experience-rated tax has declined substantially over the past several years. In many states, less than 50 percent of UI payments are now experience-rated. As a result, an increasing number of employers are paying the maximum UI tax rate. When their use of the system exceeds the amount they pay into the trust fund in taxes, the additional cost is spread among all employers regardless of employment record. This system of cross-subsidization at times has encouraged some employers to take advantage of easy access to UI benefits as an additional source of income for their workers in planning layoffs.

  There is, of course, a case for some spreading of the cost to assist firms in cyclically sensitive industries. However, the greater the spread between the minimum and maximum tax rates, the greater the incentive for the employer to manage work force changes efficiently.

Figure 25

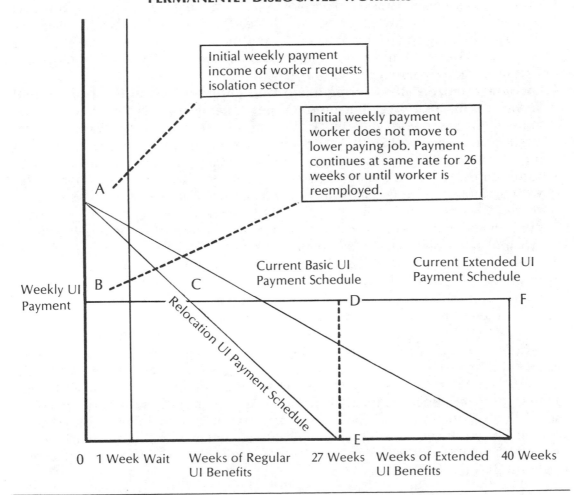

RELOCATION INCENTIVE PROGRAM FOR OLDER PERMANENTLY DISLOCATED WORKERS

USING EXISTING PROGRAMS TO TARGET SUPPORT

Improving UI's efficiency alone will mean little unless ways can be found to broaden the system's scope beyond simple short-term income support. A substantial number of displaced workers exhaust their UI benefits before ever finding new employment. The question is whether or not UI itself can be used to speed up the process and possibly even improve the quality of adjustment.

CED recommends that the following reforms be considered as ways of simultaneously broadening UI's scope and targeting assistance to displaced workers:

- **Provide the option to permanently displaced workers to continue to collect some UI benefits if they suffer earnings losses upon reemployment.** This option might take the form of a temporary, phased-in payment that would be chargeable under the current UI system to the old employer, and paid in lieu of regular UI benefits for a fixed period of time following the start of a new job.[4]

  For example, UI benefits could continue to be paid at a declining rate, provided the wage rate for the new job was lower—perhaps 10 to 20 percent lower—than the rate for the job from which he or she was displaced. Eligibility for selecting this option could be restricted to those affected by discrete structural economic change, such as a plant closing. It could also be restricted to those likely to have the greatest difficulty in finding new employment, for example, older workers with ten or more years of tenure in their lost job. (See page 43.)

  The reemployment incentive could be structured in any number of ways and could, for example, fall within the twenty-six weeks of regular UI payments or extend beyond (Figure 25). The important point is that the incentive should not be structured as a wage subsidy to employers, or as a means of simply encouraging people to move to lower-paying jobs. Instead, the incentive should provide a means of helping speed the process of adjustment for workers whose jobs have been permanently eliminated and who are unable or unlikely to find employment starting at or above their former wage.

- **Encourage more states to experiment with different uses of the Employment Service as a means of targeting support to permanently displaced workers.** Despite general dissatisfaction with the quality of service delivery provided by the Employment Service (ES), some states have succeeded in making ES a source of useful information on jobs markets and individual performance assessments. In some states, ES also plays an important role in helping structure programs for workers and communities affected by plant closings. These experiences should be shared with other states, and broader application of new technologies such as "validity generalization," capable of providing accurate assessment of individual job applicant potential, should be encouraged.[5]

Other reforms seeking broad changes in the ways that UI and ES are funded are beginning to be discussed. Some critics of the current system have suggested that program administration and service delivery would be improved if the exclusive reliance on employer contributions were dropped and employees were required to contribute to the UI trust fund. Other proposals have been made to privatize ES.[6]

These broader proposals should be examined. Five states, for example, now require employee contributions to UI, but very little is known about the administration or outcomes of these programs. Obviously, any attempt to broaden UI's scope beyond short-term income maintenance is bound to raise the subject of financing, especially given the weak fiscal position of many state unemployment funds. What we are saying here is that less ambitious but still effective changes can be made within the general framework of the current system to improve UI's efficiency and selectively target support to displaced workers.

COORDINATING FEDERAL, STATE, AND LOCAL PROGRAMS

Public programs almost always lack coordination, particularly when responsibilities are divided between federal, state, and local jurisdictions. Certain problems, however, call out for better coordinated responses. For example, the problems encountered by displaced workers require state and federal coordination of the Job Training Partnership Act (JTPA) and UI, as well as economic renewal and development programs, and local attention to specific instances of job loss. Coordination among these programs and their counterparts in the private sector is especially crucial when assistance is focused on events like plant closings which affect individuals and their communities.

In the past, coordination, while broadly proclaimed in statutes, has not occurred. Congress has not provided adequate incentives for coordination, and, too often, agencies viewing coordination as a threat have resisted.

TECHNICAL ASSISTANCE

Much of the credit for creativity in this area belongs to the various state governments that have recognized the efficacy of early intervention and cooperation. A number of states, for example, have established rapid response teams to identify and track commercial firms facing financial or competitive hardship. Technical assistance may be offered to help these firms refinance or restructure their businesses. States like

---

REEMPLOYMENT INCENTIVES IN UNEMPLOYMENT INSURANCE

How the reemployment incentive option might work is shown in Figure 25. This program can be designed so that the cost to the employer is less than the taxes which would be charged if the employee remained on UI for the entire twenty-six weeks of the basic UI program. In general, in the case of a plant closing in a local labor market in a high unemployment area, it is likely that most older permanently displaced workers will remain on the basic UI program for most of the twenty-six weeks. The relocation incentive provides the worker with a strong initial incentive to reemployment. At the same time, since the area under ABC is less than the area under CDE, the cost of the program is less than it would be if the worker remained on basic UI for twenty-six weeks hoping that the plant would reopen.

The worker could be permitted to take up to eight weeks to decide whether to exercise the option. Since the UI payment schedule declines over time, the longer the time he or she takes to elect for the option and move to the new job, the lower the UI payment.

Figure 25 also demonstrates how the same approach could be applied for a longer period of time, through the additional thirteen weeks usually available under extended UI benefits. The scheme would work very much the same as when the option paid benefits for up to twenty-six weeks. If payments are made for up to forty weeks, the worker will have a longer time to get on-the-job experience and training to raise his or her salary to its previous level. On the other hand, there is more likelihood that payments will be made to workers who would have moved to other jobs without the reemployment incentive option.

Massachusetts and California offer a variety of programs aimed at helping firms successfully adjust to market changes. Massachusetts, for example, has recently established a program offering mature industries low-cost financing for new product development.[7] States have also established university research parks to stimulate the development of new technology and job creation.

These are not exactly uncontroversial programs. Many are criticized as unwarranted state intrusions into the marketplace. Some of the programs are clearly experimental. But states that are pioneers in this area consider the risks worth taking. For them, the issue of structural changes in markets is too closely related to economic development to overlook timely interventions aimed at assisting business development or failure.

THE DISLOCATED WORKER PROVISIONS
OF THE JOB TRAINING PARTNERSHIP ACT

Far less controversial are the efforts states are taking to provide reemployment assistance to workers displaced by plant closings and other actions resulting in the permanent elimination of jobs. To this end, states are being assisted by the Job Training Partnership Act which Congress passed in 1982 to replace the Comprehensive Employment and Training Act (CETA) as the nation's primary federally funded training program. While many provisions of JTPA replaced or modified existing programs, Title III of the Act authorized an entirely new program to assist experienced workers who have permanently lost their jobs due to technology, foreign competition, or other structural changes in the economy.

The most salient feature of Title III is its flexibility. States have been given very broad authority over who is served, how the program is planned and administered, how resources are distributed, and what services will be provided. Programs can be organized in response to crisis situations, such as a major plant closing, or tailored for specific industries statewide, or targeted to high unemployment communities.

Three features of Title III are especially noteworthy:

- *No presumptive deliverers.* Title III is unusual in that, except for some review and consultation requirements, there are almost no federal mandates regarding how the program is to be delivered. States are given the option to involve business management, labor, private industry councils, community organizations, local governments, state agencies, and other entities in the programs.

- *Versatility.* A very wide range of services is authorized, including training, counseling, job search, transportation, social services, relocation assistance, and other activities. The principal federal requirement is that at least 35 percent of total federal and nonfederal matching funds (that states must provide from public or private sources) must be spent on training or related services.

- *Link to Unemployment Insurance system.* Individuals enrolled in JTPA training, which is directly related to state-identified job opportunities, are not required to be actively seeking employment during their training period. Nor do they have to accept jobs referred by the Employment Service if the acceptance of such a job would interrupt their retraining for the state-identified job opportunities.

In general, because experience with displaced workers is very limited, the intent of the law is to give states the opportunity to experiment with different approaches. In the first year or two of the program, many states played a more or less passive role, responding only after the initiative had been taken in the private sector to establish a labor-management program following the announcement of a plant closing. Even then the public response was mostly confined to the administrative handling of grant

ELEMENTS OF A WORKER ASSISTANCE CENTER

Worker assistance centers can have many forms, targeted to address the specific needs and circumstances of the affected community. Many centers are established to provide temporary *transition assistance* to a specific population of workers faced with an imminent layoff or plant closing. Such assistance centers are generally located within the plant site. Other worker assistance centers may be established as *community intervention* centers, to reach out to a neighborhood facing economic decline or a gradually deteriorating employment base. Still other assistance centers may act as *community laboratories,* offering workspace and facilities for small business development.

Whatever the size, form, or intended objectives of the center, worker assistance centers tend to incorporate a few basic ingredients:

The first is *collaboration* between public and private sectors, management and union, local social service agencies, and schools. Successful worker assistance centers are those that can integrate the resources of many different organizations, including perhaps the local Private Industry Council, funds from JTPA, vocational technical schools, local hospitals, area employers, union organizations, and so on.

Second, there must be an appropriate *sequencing of services* offered to assistance center participants.

- Enrollees should participate in *screening* to identify personal strengths, skills, and career objectives. A needs assessment can identify special individual or family needs and can involve testing for entrepreneurial ability, educational needs, and so on.

- Many assistance centers also offer one-on-one *counseling,* and can make referrals for therapeutic services or social services for participants.

- Following the initial screening, participants may receive in-house *training,* or may be referred to local vocational technical classes, on-the-job training, or any number of other educational services to update their skills base or develop new skills. Often local communities, employers, or state programs will offer special services for affected workers, such as tuition assistance for job training or academic instruction, or subsidized on-the-job training.

- Some centers also include a *business incubation* component, offering inexpensive workspace and shared facilities to help participants launch their own businesses. Local lawyers and business leaders may volunteer at the business incubation centers, offering their expertise to the entrepreneurs. State venture capital for investment in such businesses is available in some areas, while other centers rely on private venture capital funds.

- Worker assistance centers then provide *placement* services ranging from workshops in job search skills, to job banks and employment hotlines. The centers often work closely with local employers, and provide ongoing support for participants seeking employment.

In addition to collaboration and an appropriate sequencing of services, the best worker assistance centers are those which can offer

(continued next page)

> *individualized* help throughout the entire employment transition process. Invervention may begin with the announcement of a shutdown and continue for several months after the plant is closed. A community-based center may operate on a more permanent basis, reaching out to improve the economic health of an entire neighborhood or town.

applications.[8]

This slow start-up experienced by many states and a large carry-over of unspent funds is characteristic of many past federal efforts where Washington supplies the funds and the responsibility for implementation is delegated to state and local governments.

There is evidence now that both state and local agencies are becoming more actively involved as their experience grows in planning and implementing community-based programs like employee assistance centers. These centers are an especially positive example of company-union-community cooperation targeted to groups of workers drawn from local plant facilities. The elements of a model assistance center are described on page 45. The box on page 47 provides an example of such a cooperative effort, involving the closure of Allied-Signal's Prestolite Battery plant. The more active public involvement also appears to be taking on a strongly decentralized character with private industry councils or other local agencies assuming greater control and resisting direct state intervention in local employment and training issues. However, the push and pull between states and their localities will continue, with some states continuing to experiment with direct intervention. California, Massachusetts, and South Carolina, for example, are expanding the role of their rapid response teams to provide technical assistance in training and job search.[9]

Three pressing problems relating to the design and implementation of the Title III dislocated worker programs require attention. The first problem is that more states and localities need to be prepared for quick, effective response to requests for assistance. Broader use could be made of rapid response teams to identify potential plant closings and large layoffs. Simple, preferably informal information-gathering on the health of firms would enable state and local agencies to get a head start on organizing assistance. The less formal and obtrusive the intelligence system, the more effective it usually is. The Canadian government's Industrial Adjustment Service, widely hailed for its effectiveness in assisting firms and workers, collects information about impending layoffs by word of mouth, by close monitoring of business journals and newspapers, and by continued calls on businesses and unions in local areas.[10]

Furthermore, many states and localities are unprepared for quick, effective response because they are unfamiliar with the role they are being asked to play as a catalyst for labor-management cooperation. The Department of Labor has recently stepped in to provide direction on this point by offering a limited number of states the opportunity to learn first hand about the Canadian experience. If this initiative proves worthwhile, the opportunity should be made available to other states as well. Federal direction should also be used to raise the visibility of JTPA in both the public and private sectors, and to make technical assistance widely available, drawing on the good and bad experiences of already established Title III programs.

Second, better data collection and outcome measurements need to be undertaken. Title III programs, in particular, suffer from a paucity of reliable information on their effectiveness. Although some tentative measurements have been made on programs that are still very recent, the danger exists that because Title III is such a small

COLLABORATION FOR WORKER ASSISTANCE

When Allied-Signal closed the Prestolite Battery Plant in Vincennes, Indiana, Allied and United Auto Workers (UAW) initiated a joint project to assist the 180 workers who were to lose their jobs.

Allied's Electronics and Instrumentation Sector provided facilities at the plant and sufficient staff to establish a worker assistance center. Region 3 of the UAW, through their JTPA Federal Discretionary grant, provided the resources for on-the-job training, re-training, and emergency assistance to the families of workers affected by the closure. Allied also provided funding to assist those workers who resided in Illinois. The local Private Industry Council participated by conducting job search workshops and initial interviews for the workers.

The project, co-chaired and administered by the company and union staff, provided job transition assistance from the time of the announced closure for over six months after the shutdown.

part of overall JTPA funding, little attention and fewer resources will be directed to its evaluation.[11] If that happens, we will have lost one of the best opportunities for identifying what can be done to help displaced workers adjust to change. It would, for example, be extremely useful to know more about (1) the different groups of displaced workers being served, (2) what industries and occupations these workers come from and go to when reemployed, (3) whether workers most in need are being helped, (4) which training or support programs appear to facilitate reemployment for which target populations and under what conditions, and (5) what the subsequent labor market experience of program participants is over time.

Finally, Congress and the Administration need to demonstrate a firmer commitment to JTPA funding. Although Title III represents the nation's premier job training effort for dislocated workers, it is funded at a level permitting it to reach a relatively small percentage of those eligible. Last year, Title III programs served only about 178,000 participants.[12] Even at this level, cuts in federal spending have been budgeted for program years 1986 and 1987.[13] Budget deficit pressures played less of a role in persuading lawmakers to make these cuts than did the fact that appropriated funds were simply not being used up. Many states either have been slow in setting up displaced worker programs or have obligated funds faster than they have been able to spend them. As a result, there has been a large overall carry-over of unspent funds.[14]

States that were successful in establishing programs early are now faced with the need to cut back on their levels of support. There is evidence, for example, that some states are reducing the number of state-supported regional employment assistance centers or requiring private-sector payment for services rendered at these centers. Other states are reported to be cutting back on programs tailored to specific groups of displaced workers and relying more on conventional training services. Still others may find it increasingly difficult to support plant-based assistance centers.[15]

As states gain more experience in setting up displaced worker programs, the carry-over of unspent funds will be eliminated, demonstrating the need for increased appropriations. In the meanwhile, states that are in a position to provide supplemental funding should do so as an expression of their continued commitment. The Department of Labor should also ease the requirements for obtaining federal discretionary grants in support of already established programs threatened with termination for lack of formula funds.

Longer-term JTPA funding has to be stabilized, either through multi-year commitments or by finding other sources of Title III funding to supplement or replace general revenues.

TRADE ADJUSTMENT ASSISTANCE

Trade adjustment assistance (TAA) was created under the Trade Expansion Act of 1962 as a means of compensating for the potentially large losses which firms and workers in import-competing industries might bear as a result of tariff reductions negotiated during the Kennedy Round. The program offered income maintenance benefits, training, relocation, and job-search assistance to workers losing their jobs to imports. Employers were also entitled to financial assistance to improve competitiveness and to enter new businesses. Under the initial program, eligibility for assistance was explicitly linked to increased imports which were "in major part" the result of trade agreement concessions. In 1974, this linkage was removed, and workers became eligible for adjustment assistance if trade alone, whether related to a tariff reduction or not, "contributed importantly" to the loss of employment.[16]

TAA's costs and structure came under heavy criticism following the 1974 amendments. Costs grew from $147 million in 1976 to $1.6 billion in 1980, largely as a result of trade problems in the auto and steel industries. In addition, the program allowed a kind of unemployment "double dipping" by paying trade assistance at the same time that a worker was drawing regular unemployment compensation benefits. Eligible workers could, therefore, receive 70 percent of their weekly wage for up to seventy-eight weeks. Such generous cash allowances alone would not have been enough to draw the fire of opponents were it not for the fact that many TAA recipients were found to have returned to work for their former employers.[17] This raised the issue of equity: if these workers were not suffering the permanent loss of a job, their claim to special treatment was seriously undermined.

Changes made by Congress in 1981 reduced benefit payments and restricted them to workers who had exhausted regular unemployment benefits. Congress also tied additional TAA payments to enrollment in a retraining program. These changes helped send the program's costs plummeting from $1.4 billion in 1981 to $109 million in 1982 and about $54 million in each subsequent year.[18]

However, the 1981 legislation did little to change the program's dismal record in helping displaced workers find new employment. While the fraction of all workers receiving TAA benefits who entered retraining programs increased sharply (from 3.8 percent in FY 1977 to 1981, to 31.3 percent in FY 1982 to 1984), the percentage obtaining jobs for which their retraining qualified them fell (from 7.6 percent to 4.1 percent).[19] It remains to be seen whether or not a legislative requirement added in 1986, requiring that eligible workers be in a job-search or training program in order to receive benefit payments, improves this record.

Even if it could be made more structurally sound, TAA remains a fundamentally flawed program. It has served neither to stem protectionist pressures nor to promote adjustment. Furthermore, inability to satisfy the equity issue has become increasingly apparent at a time when structural changes are affecting a broad spectrum of workers. Adjustment assistance for trade-displaced workers alone can be justified only in the absence of programs serving displaced workers in general.[20] **The causes of displacement, as we have seen, are frequently less significant than the effects suffered by workers experiencing the permanent loss of their jobs. Adjustment assistance, therefore, should be both broad enough to include a variety of causes and targeted to those workers suffering the greatest hardship.**

EDUCATION REFORM

All the evidence regarding the quality of adjustment experience and the changing structure of occupations highlights the importance of education. The prospects for shorter periods of joblessness and greater recovery of earnings upon reemployment improve for all groups of displaced workers the higher their education attainment. In addition, the mix of occupations in both the services and manufacturing sectors is shifting away from employment requiring only minimum levels of skill or education. Occupations requiring a college education or post-secondary technical training head the list of fastest growing occupations over the next decade and are expected to account for 6.2 million of the 16 million jobs projected to be added from 1984 to 1995.[21]

It is not that low-skilled jobs are expected to disappear. We know, for example, that there are large numbers of such jobs in the services sector. However, these are mostly low-paying and part-time or temporary forms of employment. The better-paying jobs in both the services-producing and goods-producing sectors are increasingly to be found in the professional and managerial occupations. Even in manufacturing, the blue-collar jobs that are being eliminated are, for the most part, being replaced by white-collar employment.

This generally positive shift in the structure of occupations toward higher-skilled, higher-paying jobs will clearly benefit certain individuals, while putting others at a disadvantage. The two groups most at risk are older workers with low skills and educational levels who are displaced from high-paying jobs, and young, poorly educated workers with little or no work force experience.

In *Investing in Our Children: Business and the Public Schools,* CED calls attention to the direct impact that education has on employment and productivity.[22] We also urge a response to the following warning signals:

- Employers in both large and small businesses decry the lack of preparation for work among the nation's high school graduates. Too many students lack reading, writing, and mathematical skills, positive attitudes toward work, and appropriate behavior on the job. In addition, they have not learned how to learn, how to solve problems, make decisions, or set priorities. Many high school graduates are virtually unemployable, even at today's minimum wage.

- Well over one-quarter of the nation's youth never finish high school. Another quarter graduate without even the minimal skill requirements, and even those who go on to higher education need remedial reading and writing courses, which about two-thirds of U.S. colleges now provide.

- Nearly 13 percent of all seventeen-year-olds still enrolled in school are functionally illiterate, and 44 percent are marginally literate. Among students who drop out, an estimated 60 percent are functionally illiterate.

The policy statement recommends numerous ways schools can better prepare students for the changing workplace, and encourages a "bottom-up" strategy focused on the individual school — its students, teachers, and administrators — and the community it serves. Although the statement describes in detail those skills that employers are seeking and includes recommendations for curriculum changes, more rigorous standards, and performance measures, the heart of its concern is with improving the instructional process and the interaction between student and teacher. To this end the statement places special emphasis on ways of motivating the best to teach and on improving school management, possibly by applying lessons from the business world on handling professional employees and utilizing resources more effectively.

Adult education presents different types of challenges. It is not clear, for example, whether or not displaced workers gain more from basic education, classroom skills training, or on-the-job training (OJT). The mostly tentative findings to date show that OJT has the highest placement rate, while classroom training yields the higher post-program wage.[23] The fact that displaced workers tend to change occupations at a higher rate than most other workers suggests that educational support programs might be particularly useful. Finally, even highly educated workers in technical occupations like engineering require continuing education to prevent the obsolescence of their skills, especially when they become displaced and have to compete in the job market with recent graduates.

CHAPTER V:
CONCLUSION

So far the debate over structural economic change has been argued at the extremes: America is either suffering long-term decline, reversible only by protectionist measures, or the country is doing just fine and will continue to do so if markets are kept free from any intervention. Little wonder that most people, and policy makers in particular, are left with an uneasy feeling about the effects of change on American industry and jobs.

In this policy statement we have attempted to demonstrate that there is a middle ground in which the existence of problems and the inherent strengths of the marketplace are both recognized. CED's position is based on more than a simple desire to shun extremes. Instead, we are convinced that the direction of economic change is positive as long as the dual challenges of competitiveness and adjustment are met. Neither extreme permits this to occur because each focuses on only one or the other of these challenges.

CED's position is also based on its belief that the structural changes in markets have coincided with similarly fundamental changes in the roles of government and private industry. For government, the change stems from the limitations imposed by huge federal budget deficits, as well as from the disenchantment with the ability of massive spending programs to accomplish their goals. For industry, change comes from the realization that "business as usual" can mean disaster in an environment made intensely competitive by changes in technology and demand, and by the entry of new rivals into markets formerly dominated by the United States.

It is in this context that the debate over the effects of change is taking place, creating uncertainty about the future of American industry and the American worker. What we have attempted to demonstrate is that structural changes in markets create both opportunity and hardship, and that it is the responsibility of both the public and private sectors to assist the adjustment of people from old to new work. The fact of this adjustment is made possible by the extraordinary job-generating capacity of the American economy. This strength, unusual when compared to other countries, is the reason why the majority of displaced American workers go on to new opportunities. However, for the smaller yet sizable number of workers who are unable to make this transition without great difficulty, special support mechanisms are needed.

The adjustment challenge presents the private sector with an unusual opportunity to preempt the need for federal plant-closing legislation and to demonstrate the economic and social desirability of flexible labor markets. No amount of warning about the damage resulting from mandated restrictions on capital mobility will make up for the lack of continued commitment to voluntary action on such measures as advance notice, severance pay, or other support programs.

Adjustment also presents the opportunity to rethink the use of public programs, like Unemployment Insurance, which is now addressed primarily to temporary rather than permanent job loss, and to reexamine the commitment to job training and other forms of targeted employment assistance. Most of the hardship experienced by displaced workers results from mismatches between job need and job opportunity. The responsibility for reducing the inequities created by such hardship belongs to government. The belief in equality of opportunity, after all, is the very warp of our social fabric.

Memoranda of Comment, Reservation, or Dissent

Page 3, FLETCHER L. BYROM.

Looking to the longer term, evidence is strong that preschool education for three- and four-year olds, particularly disadvantaged children, will ensure a significant increase in qualified new entrants to the work force in a period of fifteen to twenty years after such exposure. This offers the further advantage of additional significantly cost-effective societal benefit.

Page 36, WILLIAM C. GREENOUGH, with which PHILIP KLUTZNICK and JOHN SAGAN have asked to be associated.

The CED's emphasis on portable, employment-bridging employee benefit plans is refreshing, after one-half century of using such plans in America as "golden chains" to "tie our employees to us." As the policy statement notes, plans still need to be restructured to eliminate the penalties and gaps in coverage suffered by mobile employees. Perhaps a new goal might be sought, that of neutral benefit plans designed to help attract an adequate supply of able employees during good times but flexible enough to allow parting with employees fairly and perhaps generously when retrenching must occur.

This objective would require greater attention to effective bridging between employments for life insurance, medical, and disability benefit provision. And it would require more use of defined contribution plans or correction of a major defect in most defined benefit plans that freeze at a low level the benefit for an employee who leaves much before normal retirement age.

The CED statement wisely recommends eliminating disincentives to early retirement; it might go farther and recommend sweetening early retirement provisions as a fair and acceptable way to reduce labor force when needed.

Page 3, RODERICK M. HILLS.

Care must of course be taken not to force subsidies on a community where economic reality means the community must shrink.

Page 2 and page 28, SIDNEY J. WEINBERG, JR., with which PHILIP KLUTZNICK and WILLIAM MAY have asked to be associated.

Flexibility in worker compensation is a good objective. I believe it would be wise for most or all of that compensation to be tied to the performance or productivity of the individual worker or his or her work unit, rather than to the performance of the corporation as a whole. Relating compensation to criteria closer to the individual would have a more favorable effect on worker performance and would be a fairer method of rewarding excellence.

FOOTNOTES
CHAPTER II

1. Valerie A. Personick, "A Second Look at Industry Output and Employment Trends Through 1995," *Monthly Labor Review* 108: 11 (November 1985), p. 26.

2. U.S. Bureau of Labor Statistics (BLS) *Trends in Manufacturing: A Chartbook*, (Washington, D.C. April 1985), pp. 2-3. Also, Ronald E. Kutscher and Valerie A. Personick, "Deindustrialization and the Shift to Services," in *Monthly Labor Review* (June 1986), p. 3. Manufacturing output declined 1.5 percent in the second quarter 1986, after continuing to post gains in 1985 and in the first quarter 1986.

3. BLS, Office of Productivity and Technology.

4. Between 1973 and 1985, manufacturing share of real GNP dropped from 22.1 percent to 21.7 percent; employment share dropped from 26.3 percent to 20 percent.

5. Marvin Kosters, "Free Markets Bring Change and Growth," *Challenge* 29: 1 (special issue, March-April 1986), p. 58.

6. Kutscher and Personick, *Deindustrialization,* pp. 9-10.

7. BLS, Division of Employment and Unemployment Analysis.

8. Service-producing industries include all government jobs and five private service-producing sectors: transportation and public utilities, wholesale trade, retail trade, finance, insurance and real estate, and services.

9. BLS, Division of Employment Services.

10. See, for example, Barry Bluestone and Bennett Harrison, *The Deindustrialization of America* (New York: Basic Books, Inc., 1982); also Bob Kuttner, "The Declining Middle," *The Atlantic Monthly* (July 1983), pp. 60-72.

11. Kosters, "Free Markets Bring Change," pp. 56-57.

12. Ronald E. Kutscher, "Employment Growth in the United States" (Paper presented to National Council on Employment Policy, Washington, D.C., April 17, 1986), pp.6-9.

13. Michael Urquhart examined employment shifts between sectors to discover whether or not "new" employees in services previously worked in goods or agriculture or did not work at all the prior year. His conclusion was that most of the intersectoral movement taking place occurred from services to goods. Employment growth in the service sector, in other words, "stemmed largely from expansion of the labor force, particularly the increased participation of women." Urquhart used data from the March 1978-79 matched file of the CPS to compare a person's employment status in 1977 to his or her status in 1978. See Michael Urquhart, "The Employment Shift to Services: Where Did It Come From?" *Monthly Labor Review* (April 1984), pp. 15-22.

14. The average annual increase for women 16 years and older was 7.2 percent per year, compared to 6.1 percent per year for all workers 16 years and older. Based on BLS unpublished data on median weekly earnings of wage and salary workers who usually work full-time, by selected characteristics, selected dates 1967 to 1986.

15. Over the 5 years ending in June 1986, compensation grew at an average annual compounded rate of 5.6 percent in service producing industries, 5.0 percent in goods producing industries, and 5.2 percent in manufacturing. Based on the Employment Costs Index (ECI) for private industry only, BLS, June 1986. The ECI measures changes in compensation costs, which include wages, salaries and employer costs for employee benefits.

16. "The occupational classification system in the CPS changed in 1983, so comparable data for 1983-forward are not available. Nor are strictly comparable data available for periods earlier than 1972" (Kutscher, "Employment Growth in the United States," p. 12). An examination of the new classification system shows similar movement occurring between 1983 and 1985, although operatives did recover some of their recessionary losses.

17. George T. Silvestri and John M. Lukasiewicz, "Occupational Employment Projections: The 1984-95 Outlook," *Monthly Labor Review* (November 1985), pp. 42-43.

18. Urquhart, "The Employment Shift to Services," pp. 16 and 18.

19. See Paul O. Flaim and Ellen Sehgal, "Displaced Workers of 1979-83: How Well Have They Fared?" *Monthly Labor Review* (June 1985). The article analyzed data compiled from a special survey sponsored by the Department of Labor's Employment and Training Administration and conducted in January 1984 as a supplement to the Current Population Survey (CPS). Information provided in this section on displaced workers is drawn from Flaim and Sehgal's analysis as well as the analysis of the same data done by Michael Podgursky and Paul Swain, "Labor Market Adjustment and Job Displacement: Evidence From the January, 1984 Displaced Worker Survey," for the Bureau of International Labor Affairs, U.S. Department of Labor (Washington, D.C.: Government Printing Office, January 1986). Podgursky and Swain focused on the same causes of displacement, but dropped the tenure criterion in order to enlarge their sample and cover all workers aged 20-61 who were formerly employed full-time in wage and salary jobs.

20. The BLS used a 3-year tenure criterion as a means of further distinguishing displaced workers from other job losers. Displaced workers, in other words, are unusual not only with regard to the permanence of their job loss, but also by virtue of the considerable amount of years and skills development invested in their former jobs, making the "prospects for their reemployment in similar jobs rather dim" (Flaim and Sehgal, *Displaced Workers of 1979-83*, p. 2).

21. "Reemployment Increases Among Displaced Workers," BLS *News*, October 14, 1986. The BLS recently completed a second survey of workers displaced from their jobs between 1981 and 1986. The findings of the two surveys are remarkably similar, except for the high proportion of workers reemployed in the more recent period. A little over 67 percent of the 5.1 million workers displaced from their jobs between 1981 and 1986 had found new employment as of January 1986; nearly 18 percent were still unemployed, while 15 percent had left the labor force. See BLS, "Analysis of Mass Layoff Data," (unpublished).

CHAPTER III

1. Note: For more on this topic, see CED policy statement: *Productivity Policy: Key to the Nation's Economic Future*, April 1983. See also William J. Baumol and Kenneth McLennan, *Productivity Growth and U.S. Competitiveness*, 1985; and Otto Eckstein, Christopher Caton, Roger Brinner, and Peter Duprey, *The DRI Report on U.S. Manufacturing Industries* (1984).

2. Martin L. Weitzman, *The Share Economy: Conquering Stagflation* (Cambridge, Massachusetts: Harvard University Press, 1984). According to Weitzman, the standard practice of paying workers a fixed wage, regardless of whether a company is doing well or poorly, throws the entire burden of adjustment in an economy on employment and on prices.

3. Audrey Freedman, "The New Look in Wage Policy and Employee Relations," The Conference Board (New York: The Conference Board, 1985).

4. Freedman, "The New Look in Wage Policy," pp. 1-4.

5. The Scanlon Plan and other forms of tailored reward system approaches to compensation are discussed in "Reward Systems and Productivity: A Final Report For The White House Conference on Productivity" (Washington, D.C.: American Productivity Center, 1983).

6. The need for greater flexibility, especially labor market flexibility, is becoming widely recognized in OECD countries. See "Labour Market Flexibility: A Controversial Issue," *The OECD Observer*, No. 141, (July 1986), p.

12. See "United States-Japan Comparative Study of Employment Adjustment," U.S. Department of Labor, Bureau of International Labor Affairs, March 1985, for comparison of Japanese/American adjustment experiences.

See also

7. "American Workers Don't Get Around Much Anymore," *Business Week* (October 28, 1985), p. 94.

8. Flaim and Sehgal, "Displaced Workers of 1979-83," p. 6

9. Flaim and Sehgal, "Displaced Workers of 1979-83," pp. 9 and 13.

10. "Are Service Jobs Good Jobs?" *Fortune* III: 11 (June 10, 1985), p. 41.

11. Anthony P. Carnevale and Harold Goldstein, *Employee Training: Its Changing Role and Analysis of New Data* (Washington, D.C.), pp. 32-36. See also Seymour Lusterman, *Trends in Corporate Education and Training* (Washington, D.C.: 1985), p. 4; and *Employee Educational Assistance: Who Pays, Who Benefits,* The American Society for Training and Development (Washington, D.C.: May 1985).

12. Ronald E. Berenbeim, *Company Programs to Ease the Impact of Shutdowns* (New York: The Conference Board, 1986), p. 8. See also "GAO's Preliminary Analysis of U.S. Business Closures and Permanent Layoffs During 1983 and 1984," (Washington, D.C.: U.S. General Accounting Office (GAO), Human Resources Division, April 1986), and "Plant Closing: Advance Notice and Rapid Response — Special Report," Office of Technology Assessment, September 1986.

13. Berenbeim, *Company Programs to Ease the Impact of Shutdowns,* pp. 7-8.

14. The Business Roundtable, "Plant Closings: A Position Paper" (June 1983). The National Alliance of Business has also developed company guidelines for plant closings. In addition, see "Managing Plant Closings and Occupational Readjustment: An Employer's Guide," ed. Richard P. Swigart (Washington, D.C.: National Center on Occupational Readjustment, Inc., September 1984).

CHAPTER IV

1. Seong H. Park, "Interrelated Nature of Budget Deficits and Trade Deficits," an unpublished paper prepared for the Committee for Economic Development (CED), 1986. See also CED policy statement, *Fighting Federal Deficits: The Time for Hard Choices* (New York: 1984).

2. George N. Hatsopoulos and Steven H. Brooks, "The Gap in the Cost of Capital: Causes, Effects, and Remedies" *Technology and Economic Policy,* edited by Ralph Landau and Dale Jorgenson (1986).

3. CED policy statement, *Strategy for U.S. Industrial Competitiveness* (New York: April 1984), Chapter 4.

4. See Wayne Zajac, "Alternative Uses of Unemployment Insurance," p. 40. Luxembourg and the Netherlands provide wage supplements to unemployed individuals who accept employment at lower wages than they earned in their prior employment. Note: The United States is now experimenting with wage bonuses in Illinois and New Jersey.

5. See Zajac, "Alternative Uses of Unemployment Insurance," Chapter 3, for examples of state initiatives for retraining and relocation assistance for dislocated workers.

6. See statement by Burton L. Carlson before the Secretary of Labor's Task Force on Economic Adjustment and Worker Dislocation, February 5, 1986. See also National Alliance for Business Ad Hoc Business Group working committee, "Exploring Employment Service Options" an unpublished working draft; and the National Council on Employment Policy, *Policy Statement on the United States Employment Service,* (May 1985).

7. Neal R. Peirce and Carol Steinbach, "Massachusetts, After Going from Rags to Riches, Looks to Spread the Wealth," *National Journal* 17:21 (May 25, 1985), p. 1231.

8. Kevin Balfe and Ruth Fedrau, "Summary Report: Review and Analysis of Company/Union Sponsored Comprehensive Displaced Worker Assistance Centers Receiving JTPA Title III Support" (April 1986), pp. 7-8.

9. Balfe and Fedrau, "Review of Company/Union Sponsored Centers," p. 8.

10. William L. Batt, Jr. "Canada's Good Example with Displaced Workers," *Harvard Business Review* 61 : 4 (July-August 1983).

11. *GAO, Job Training Partnership Act: Data Collection Efforts and Needs,* March 1986.

12. GAO, *Dislocated Workers: Extent of Business Closures, Layoffs, and the Public and Private Response* (Washington, D.C.: July 1986), p. 21.

13. GAO, *Dislocated Workers,* p. 20.

14. GAO, *Technology and Structural Unemployment: Reemploying Displaced Adults,* p. 165.

15. Balfe and Fedrau, *Review of Company/Union Sponsored Centers,* pp. 22-23.

16. Robert W. Bednarzik and James A. Orr, *The Effectiveness of Trade-Related Worker Adjustment Policies in the United States,* Economic Dicussion Paper 15, U.S. Department of Labor, Bureau of International Labor Affairs (February 1985), p. 6-8.

17. Charles F. Stone and Isabel V. Sawhill, "Labor Market Implications of the Growing Internationalization of the U.S. Economy," unpublished, June 1986, p. 36-37.

18. GAO, *Dislocated Workers,* p. 20.

19. Robert Z. Lawrence and Robert E. Litan, "Living with the Trade Deficit: Adjustment Strategies to Preserve Free Trade" *The Brookings Review* 4: 1, The Brookings Institution (Fall 1985), p. 10. See also "Trade Aid Doesn't Stress 'Adjustment'" *National Journal* (January 11, 1986), p. 90.

20. Steve Charnovitz, "Worker Adjustment: The Missing Ingredient in Trade Policy," *California Management Review* XXVII: 2, (Winter 1986). "Advocates of TAA never claimed that import victims were the *only* ones needing adjustment. What was claimed was that, in the absence of a dislocation program serving everyone, there was sufficient political reason to give import victims the assistance needed to restitute injury." p. 163.16. George Silvestri and John M. Lukasiewicz, "Occupational employment projections: The 1984-95 outlook," *Monthly Labor Review,* (November 1985). See Table 1 on p. 43 and Table 4 on p. 52.

21. Silvestri and Lukasiewicz, "Occupational employment projections: the 1984-95 outlook." See Table 1 on p. 43 and Table 4 on p. 52.

22. CED policy statement, *Investing in Our Children: Business and the Public Schools* (New York: 1985).

23. GAO, *Dislocated Workers,* pp. 36-37.

BIBLIOGRAPHY

A

"A Puzzlingly Poorly Productive America," World Business in *The Economist*. London: The Economist Newspaper, Ltd., March 29, 1986, p. 55.

Aarsteinsen, Barbara. "Needed: Experts to Service our Electronic Way of Life," *The New York Times*. New York: The New York Times Company, March 24, 1985, Section 12, p. 49.

Alternative Uses of Unemployment Insurance. Unemployment Insurance Service Occasional Paper #86-1, U.S. Department of Labor, Employment and Training Administration. Washington, D.C.: GPO, 1986.

Ando, Albert and Auerbach, Alan. "The Corporate Cost of Capital in Japan and the U.S.: A Comparison," Working Paper No. 1762. Cambridge, MA: National Bureau of Economic Research, October 1985.

Ano, Michael C., and Orr, James A. "Trade-sensitive Employment: Who Are the Affected Workers?" *Monthly Labor Review*, Bureau of Labor Statistics, U.S. Department of Labor. Washington, D.C.: GPO, February 1981.

Armington, Catherine. "Further Examination of Sources of Recent Employment Growth: Analysis of USEEM Data for 1976 to 1980." Washington, D.C.: The Brookings Institution, March 1983.

Armington, Catherine, and Odle, Marjorie. "Small Business — How Many Jobs?" *The Brookings Review*. Washington, D.C.: The Brookings Institution, Winter 1982, p. 14.

"Auto Output: The Best in Seven Years," *Business Week*. New York: McGraw Hill, Inc., October 21, 1985, p. 34.

B

Baldwin, Stephen E., and Donohue, Ann. "Displaced Workers: New Options for a Changing Economy," Research Report Series RR-83-17. Washington, D.C.: National Commission for Employment Policy, September 1983.

Balfe, Kevin, and Fedrau, Ruth. "Summary Report: Review and Analysis of Company/Union Sponsored Comprehensive Displaced Worker Assistance Centers Receiving JTPA Title III Support," Submitted to the Office of Technology Assessment, Congress of the United States, April 18, 1986.

Batt, William, L., Jr. "Canada's Good Example with Displaced Workers," *Harvard Business Review*. Cambridge, MA: Harvard University, July-August 1983, p. 6.

Baumol, William J., and McLennan, Kenneth. *Productivity Growth and U.S. Competitiveness*. New York: Oxford University Press, 1985.

Bednarzik, Robert W., "Layoffs and Permanent Job Losses: Workers' Traits and Cyclical Patterns," *Monthly Labor Review*, Bureau of Labor Statistics, U.S. Department of Labor. Washington, D.C.: GPO, September 1983.

Bednarzik, Robert W., and Orr, James A. *The Effectiveness of Trade-Related Worker Adjustment Policies in the United States*. Economic Discussion Paper 15, U.S. Department of Labor, Bureau of International Labor Affairs. Washington, D.C.: GPO, February 1984.

Bendick, Marc, Jr. "Workers Dislocated by Economic Change: Toward New Institutions for Midcareer Worker Transformation." Washington, D.C.: The Urban Institute, February 1982.

Bendick, Marc, Jr., and Devine, Judith Radlinski. "Workers Dislocated by Economic Change: Do They Need Federal Employment and Training Assistance?" Washington, D.C.: The Urban Institute, August 1981.

Berenbeim, Ronald E. *Company Programs to Ease the Impact of Shutdowns*. New York: The Conference Board, 1986.

Berg, Eric N. "A New World of Telecommunications Jobs," *The New York Times*. New York: The New York Times Company, March 24, 1985, Section 12, p. 48.

Berger, Joan, with Mervosh, Edward. "American Workers Don't Get Around Much Anymore," *Business Week*. New York: McGraw Hill, Inc., October 28, 1985, p. 94.

60

Berin, Barnet N. "Prevent the Mugging of Private Employee Benefits," *Across the Board.* New York: The Conference Board, December 1984, p. 52.

Block, Richard N., and McLennan, Kenneth. "Structural Economic Change and Industrial Relations in the United States' Manufacturing and Transportation Sectors: 1973-1983," Industrial Relations Research Association Research Volume entitled *Industrial Relations in a Decade of Economic Growth,* Hervey Juris, Mark Thompson, and Wilbur Daniels, Eds. Madison, Wisc.: Industrial Relations Research Association, March 1985.

Bolt, James F. "Job Security: Its Time has Come, *Harvard Business Review.* Cambridge, MA: Harvard University, November-December 1983, p. 115.

Brown, Warren. "Ford Steers New Course," *The Washington Post.* Washington, D.C.: The Washington Post Company, November 17, 1985, p. D-1.

Buss, Dale D. "Auto Firms' Blue-Collar Transfers Result in Troubles at Work, Home," *The Wall Street Journal.* New York: Dow Jones and Co., Inc., May 15, 1984, Section 12, p. 31.

C

Carlson, Burton L. Statement before the Task Force on Economic Adjustment and Worker Dislocation, February 5, 1986.

Carnevale, Anthony P., and Goldstein, Harold. *Employee Training: Its Changing Role and Analysis of New Data.* Washington, D.C.: American Society for Training and Development, 1983.

Caton, Christopher. "Some Thoughts on the Future of Manufacturing," *U.S. Long Term Review,* Katharine Kush, ed. Lexington, MA: Data Resources, Inc., Summer 1983.

Cerami, Charles A. "The Looming Worldwide Job Shortage," *The New York Times.* New York: The New York Times Company, January 13, 1985, Section 3, p. 3.

Charnovitz, Steve. "Worker Adjustment: The Missing Ingredient in Trade Policy," *California Management Review.* Vol. XXVII no. 2. Berkeley, CA: University of California, Winter 1986, p. 156-173.

Choate, Pat. *High Flex Society.* Unpublished manuscript, 1986.

Cook, Robert F., et al. "State Level Implementation of the Job Training Partnership Act." Rockville, MD: Westat, Inc., May 1984.

Cooney, Stephen. *U.S. Trade, Industrial Competitiveness and Economic Growth.* Washington, D.C.: National Association of Manufacturers, August 1985.

Corrigan, Richard. "Calling All Kids," *National Journal.* Washington, D.C.: National Journal, Inc., March 8, 1986, p. 558.

Corrigan, Richard. "Modest Proposals," *National Journal.* Washington, D.C.: Government Research Corporation, March 26, 1983, p. 664.

Corrigan, Richard. "No Smoke, No Growth? *National Journal.* Washington, D.C.: National Journal, Inc., July 27, 1985, p. 1732.

Corrigan, Richard, and Stanfield, Rochelle, L. "Casualties of Change," *National Journal.* Washington, D.C.: National Journal, Inc., February 11, 1984, p. 252.

D

Dean, Edwin; Boissevain, Harry; and Thomas, James. "Productivity and Labor Costs Trends in Manufacturing, 12 Countries," *Monthly Labor Review,* Bureau of Labor Statistics, U.S. Department of Labor. Washington, D.C.: GPO, March 1986, p. 3.

de Bernardo, Mark A. *Statement of the Chamber of Commerce of the United States* on Plant Closings and Relocations and the Labor-Management Notification and Consultation Act of 1985, H.R. 1616, to Labor-Management Relations Subcommittee and the Employment Opportunities Subcommittee of the House Committee on Education and Labor. Washington, D.C.: U.S. Chamber of Commerce, May 1985.

Demovich, Linda E. "Jobs + School = Success?" *National Journal.* Washington, D.C.: Government Research Corporation, July 16, 1983, p. 1508.

Devans, Richard M., Jr. "Displaced Workers: One Year Later," *Monthly Labor Review,* Bureau of Labor Statistics, United States Department of Labor, July 1986.

Devans, Richard M., Jr.; Leon, Carol Boyd; and Sprinkle, Debbie L. "Employment and Unemployment in 1984: A Second Year of Strong Growth in Jobs," *Employment and Unemployment: A Report on 1984*, Bureau of Labor Statistics, U.S. Department of Labor. Washington, D.C.: GPO, February 1985.

Dislocated Workers: Extent of Business Closures, Layoffs, and the Public and Private Response. United States General Accounting Office, U.S. Congress. Washington, D.C.: GPO, July 1986.

Dislocated Workers: Issues and Federal Options. Congressional Budget Office, U.S. Congress. Washington, D.C.: GPO, July 1982.

Dobrzynski, Judith H., and Peterson, Thane. "Fighting Back: It Can Work," *Business Week.* New York: McGraw Hill, Inc., August 26, 1985, p. 62.

Drucker, Peter F. "Demographics and American Economic Policy," *Toward a New U.S. Industrial Policy?* Michael L. Wachter and Susan M. Wachter, Eds. Philadelphia, Pennsylvania: University of Pennsylvania Press, 1981, pp. 237-256.

Drucker, Peter F. "Why America's Got So Many Jobs," *The Wall Street Journal.* New York: Dow Jones and Co., Inc., January 24, 1984, p. 32.

E

Economic Report of the President. Washington, D.C.: GPO, February 1986.

Eckstein, Otto, et al. *The DRI Report on U.S. Manufacturing Industries,* Data Resources, Inc. New York: McGraw Hill Book Company, 1984.

Employment and Earnings, Bureau of Labor Statistics, U.S. Department of Labor. Washington, D.C.: GPO, January 1984.

Employee Educational Assistance: Who Pays, Who Benefits. Alexandria, VA: The American Society for Training and Development, May 1985.

"Europe's Spotty Record with Job Programs," *Business Week.* New York: McGraw Hill, Inc., March 7, 1977, p. 34.

F

Feder, Barnaby J. "New Budget for Britain Focuses on Adding Jobs," *The New York Times.* New York: The New York Times Company, March 20, 1985, Section D, p. 5.

Fedrau, Ruth H. "Responses to Plant Closures and Major Reductions in Force: Private Sector and Community-based Models," ANNALS, AAPSS. Philadelphia, PA: The American Academy of Political and Social Science, September 1984.

Fedrau, Ruth H., and Balfe, Kevin. "Adapting the Workforce to Improve Productivity and International Competitiveness," Paper presented at the California Employment Training Panel Seminar on "Job Training and Economic Productivity." Washington, D.C.: National Alliance of Business, August 1984.

Fighting Federal Deficits: The Time for Hard Choices. A Statement by Research and Policy Committee of the Committee for Economic Development. Washington, D.C.: Committee for Economic Development, 1984.

Flaim, Paul O., and Sehgal, Ellen. "Displaced Workers of 1979-83: How Well Have They Fared?" *Monthly Labor Review,* Bureau of Labor Statistics, U.S. Department of Labor. Washington, D.C.: GPO, June 1985.

Freeman, Harry L. "Services Key in Two-Tier Economy," *Financier.* New York: FinEdit Ltd., vol. X, no. 2, February 1986, p. 35.

Freedman, Audrey. *The New Look in Wage Policy and Employee Relations.* New York: The Conference Board, 1985.

G

Gainer, William J. "GAO's Preliminary Analysis of U.S. Business Closures and Permanent Layoffs During 1983 and 1984." For presentation at the OTA/GAO Workshop of Plant Closings. Washington, D.C.: U.S. General Accounting Office, April 1986.

Goldman, Barbara, et al. "Findings From the San Diego Job Search and Work Experience Demonstration." New York: Manpower Demonstration Research Corporation, March 1985.

62

Greene, Richard. "Tracking Job Growth in Private Industry," *Monthly Labor Review*, Bureau of Labor Statistics, U.S. Department of Labor. Washington, D.C.: GPO, September 1982, P. 3.

Greenhouse, Steven. "U.S. Steel Closings Expected," *The New York Times*. New York: The New York Times Company, December 27, 1983, Section D. p. 1.

Gresser, Jullian, and Osterman, Andrew. "Competing with the Japanese on their own Turf," *The Wall Street Journal*. New York: Dow Jones and Co., Inc., December 2, 1985, p. 20.

H

Hatsopoulos, George N., and Brooks, Stephen H. "The Gap in the Cost of Capital: Causes, Effects, and Remedies," Reprint from *Technology and Economic Policy*, Ralph Landau and Dale Jorgenson, Eds. Cambridge, MA: Ballinger Publishing Company, 1986.

Hayes, Thomas C. "U.S. Losing Ground in Electronics," *The New York Times*. New York: The New York Times Company, March 24, 1985, Section 12, p. 1.

Hershey, Robert D., Jr. "U.S. Expected to Report Creation of 10 Million New Jobs Since '82," *The New York Times*. New York: The New York Times Company, March 24, 1985, Section 10, p. 22.

Holusha, John. "For Manufacturing Design, A Glittering New Glamour," *The New York Times*. New York: The New York Times Company, March 24, 1985, Section 10, p. 22.

"How Not To Retrain Workers." *The Washington Post*. Washington, D.C.: The Washington Post Company, November 12, 1983, p. A-18.

Hunt, H. Allan, and Hunt, Timothy L. *Human Resource Implications of Robotics*. Kalamazoo, Michigan: The W.E. Upjohn Institute for Employment Research, 1983.

I

The Industrial Policy Debate. A Congressional Budget Office Study, Congress of the United States. Washington, D.C.: GPO, December 1983.

Investing in our Children: Business and the Public Schools, A Statement by the Research and Policy Committee of the Committee for Economic Development. Washington, D.C.: Committee for Economic Development, 1985.

J

"Job Growth, Flexibility, and Security," *The OECD Observer*, no. 136. Paris, France: Organization for Economic Co-Operation and Development, September 1985.

The Job Training Partnership Act: An Analysis of Support Cost Limits and Participant Characteristics, United States General Accounting Office, U.S. Congress. Washington, D.C.: GPO, November, 1985.

Job Training Partnership Act: Data Collection Efforts and Needs, United States General Accounting Office, Briefing Report to the Chairman, Subcommittee on Employment Opportunities, Committee on Education and Labor, U.S. House of Representatives. Washington, D.C.: GPO, March 1986.

K

Kantor, Seth. "Pink Slip for this Program to Aid Jobless?" *Nation's Business*. Washington, D.C.: U.S. Chamber of Commerce, May 1983, p. 39.

Kirkland, Richard I., Jr. "Are Service Jobs Good Jobs?" *Fortune*. Los Angeles, CA: Time, Inc., June 10, 1985, p. 38.

Kolberg, William H., Ed. "The Dislocated Worker: Preparing America's Workforce for New Jobs," *National Alliance of Business*, Washington, D.C.: Seven Locks Press, 1983.

Kornblum, Annette. "Unemployment Compensation: The System Isn't Working," *Nation's Business*, Washington, D.C.: U.S. Chamber of Commerce, May 1983, p. 74.

Kosters, Marvin H. "Free Markets Bring Change and Growth," *Challenge*. Armonk, NY: ME Sharpe, Inc., March-April 1986, p. 55.

Kosters, Marvin H. "Job Changes and Displaced Workers: An Examination of Employment Adjustment Experience," *Essays in Contemporary Economic Problems, 1986,* Philip Cagan, Ed., Washington, D.C.: American Enterprise Institute, April 1986.

Kristof, Nicholas D. "Every Region Gets Into the Technology Act," *The New York Times,* New York: The New York Times Company, March 24, 1985, Section 12, p. 7.

Kutscher, Ronald E. "Employment Growth in the United States," presentation to National Council on Employment Policy, Washington, D.C. April 17, 1986.

Kuttner, Bob. "Jobs," *Alternatives: Proposals from the Democratic Left,* Irving How, Ed. Foundation for the Study of Indepedent Social Ideas, Inc. New York: Pantheon Books, 1984.

L

"Labor Market Adjustment Issues and Policy Principles for Dislocated Workers," Washington, D.C.: National Alliance of Business, November 1985.

"Labor Market Implications of the Growing International Technical Proposal of the U.S. Economy." Washington, D.C.: The Urban Institute, May 1985.

"Labour Market Flexibility: A Controversial Issue." *The OECD Observer,* no. 141. Paris, France: Organization for Economic Co-Operation and Development, July 1986, p. 12.

Lanier, Alfredo S. "Brother, Can You Spare a Job?" *Chicago.* Chicago, Illinois: Chicago Magazine — WFMT, September 1985, p. 152.

Lawrence, Robert Z. *Can America Compete?* Washington, D.C.: The Brookings Institution, 1984.

Lawrence, Robert Z. "Stubborn Demographics: The Middle Class is Alive and Well," *The New York Times.* New York: The New York Times Company, June 23, 1985, Section 3, p. 3.

Lawrence, Robert Z., and Litan, Robert E. "Living with the Trade Deficit: Adjustment Strategies to Preserve Free Trade," *The Brookings Review,* vol. 4, no. 1. Washington, D.C.: The Brookings Institution, Fall 1985, p. 3.

Leary, Thomas J. "Deindustrialization, Plant Closing Laws, and the States," *State Government,* vol. 58, no. 3. Lexington, Kentucky: The Council of State Governments, Fall 1985, pp. 113-118.

Lewis, Paul. "Europeans Try to Reduce Unemployment or Make It Pay," *The New York Times,* New York: The New York Times Company, March 31, 1985.

Lubar, Robert. "Why Unemployment Will Hang High," Fortune. Los Angeles, CA: Time, Inc., June 14, 1982, p. 114.

Lusterman, Seymour. *Trends in Corporate Education and Training.* New York: The Conference Board, 1985.

M

MacKnight, Susan. "Japan's Expanding Manufacturing Presence in the United States: A Profile." Washington, D.C.: Japan Economic Institute of America, March/April 1985.

Mazza, Jacqueline, and Mayer, Virginia. "Shutdown: A Guide for Communities Facing Plant Closings." Washington, D.C.: Northeast-Midwest Institute, January 1982.

McComas, Maggie. "Time Bombs in the 1984 Tax Act," *Fortune.* Los Angeles, CA: Time, Inc., October 15, 1984, p. 195.

McGlenahen, John S. "Getting America Back to Work," *Industry Week.* Cleveland, OH: Penton Publishing Inc., June 13, 1983, p. 36.

McLennan, Kenneth. "Policy Options to Facilitate the Reemployment of Displaced Workers: Implication for Educational and Training Institutions," Kevin Hollenbeck, Frank C. Pratzner, and Howard Rosen, Eds. Columbia, Ohio: The National Center for Research in Vocational Education, Ohio State University, 1984.

McLennan, Kenneth. "Redefining Goverment's Role in the Workplace," Washington, D.C.: National Council on Employment Policy, Symposium on Federal Intervention in the Workplace, draft for publication in 1986.

McKenzie, Richard B. *Fugitive Industry: The Economics and Politics of Reindustrialization.* Pacific Institute for Public Policy Research. Cambridge, MA: Bollinger Publishing Company, 1984.

64

McKenzie, Richard B. *What Should Be Done for Displaced Workers?* St. Louis, MO: Center for the Study of American Business, Washington University, November 1985.

McKenzie, Richard B., Ed. *Plant Closings: Public or Private Choices?* Washington, D.C.: Cato Institute, 1982.

McKenzie, Richard B., with Smith, Stephen. "'Missing Middle' Fears are Unfounded," *Financier* vol. X, no. 3. New York: FinEdit Ltd., March 1986, p. 48.

McKenzie, Richard B., with Smith, Stephen D. *The Good News About U.S. Production Jobs.* St. Louis, MO: Center for the Study of American Business, Washington University, Format Publication Number 72, February 1986.

Mellor, Earl. Data on median weekly earnings, as yet unpublished, Bureau of Labor Statistics, July 1986.

Mellor, Earl, and Stamas, George D. "Unusual Weekly Earnings: Another Look at Intergroup Differences and Basic Trends," *Monthly Labor Review,* Bureau of Labor Statistics, U.S. Department of Labor. Washington, D.C.: GPO, April 1982.

Meyer, Mitchell. *Flexible Employee Benefits Plans: Companies' Experience.* New York: The Conference Board, 1983.

"Most New Jobs are Still in Services," *Business Week.* New York: McGraw-Hill, October 21, 1985, p. 33.

Myers, Henry F. "U.S. Productivity Gains Outlook in Still Fall Short", *The Wall Street Journal.* New York: Dow Jones & Company, Inc., February 10, 1986, p. 1.

N

Noble, Kenneth B. "Study Finds 60% of 11 Million Who Lost Jobs Got New Ones," *The New York Times.* New York: The New York Times Company, February 7, 1986, Section A, p. 1.

Norwood, Janet L. "The Growth in Service Jobs," Economic Scene in *The New York Times.* New York: The New York Times Company, August 28, 1985, p. D2.

"Not by Services Alone," American Survey in *The Economist,* London: The Economist Newspaper, Ltd., July 13, 1985, p. 24.

P

Page, David A. "The Phantom Jobless," *The New York Times.* New York: The New York Times Company, August 24, 1984, Section A, p. 25.

Park, Seong H. "Interrelated Nature of Budget Deficits and Trade Deficits." Washington, D.C.: Committee for Economic Development, June 1986.

Pierce, Neal R., and Guskind, Robert. "Job Training for Hard-Core Unemployed Continues to Elude the Government," *National Journal.* Washington, D.C.: National Journal, Inc., September 28, 1985, p. 2197.

Pierce, Neal R., and Steinbach, Carol. "Massachusetts, After Going from Rags to Riches, Looks to Spread the Wealth," *National Journal.* Washington, D.C.: National Journal, Inc., May 25, 1985, p. 1227.

Personick, Valerie A. "A Second Look at Industry Output and Employment Trends Through 1995," *Monthly Labor Review,* Bureau of Labor Statistics. U.S. Government Printing Office, November 1985.

Plant Closing: Advance Notice and Rapid Response-Special Report. Office of Technology Assessment, U.S. Congress. Washington, D.C.: GPO September 1986.

"Plant Closings: A Position Paper." New York: The Business Roundtable, June 1983.

Plewes, Thomas J. "Briefing on Economic Adjustment and Worker Dislocation." Presentation to the Task Force on Economic Adjustment and Worker Dislocation, December 17, 1985.

Podgursky, Michael, and Swaim, Paul. "Labor Market Adjustment and Job Displacement: Evidence from the January, 1984 Displaced Worker Survey," Bureau of International Labor Affairs, U.S. Department of Labor. Washington, D.C.: GPO, January 1986.

Policy Statement on the United States Employment Service, National Council on Employment Policy. Washington, D.C.: National Council on Employment Policy, May 1985.

Pollack, Andrew. "Service Jobs Start to Drift Abroad, Too," *The New York Times.* New York: The New York Times Company, March 23, 1986, Section 12, p. 7.

Productivity Policy: Key to the Nation's Economic Future. A Statement by the Research and Policy Committee of the Committee for Economic Development. Washington, D.C.: Committee for Economic Development, April 1983.

R

"Reemployment Increases Among Displaced Workers," *Bureau of Labor Statistics News,* U.S. Department of Labor, Bureau of Labor Statistics. Washington, D.C.: GPO, October 14, 1986.

"Reward Systems and Productivity: A Final Report For The White House Conference on Productivity." American Productivity Center, 1983.

Rosenthal, Neal H. "The Shrinking Middle Class: Myth or Reality?" *Monthly Labor Review,* Bureau of Labor Statistics, U.S. Department of Labor. Washington, D.C.: GPO, March 1985.

Rubin, Nancy. "Laser-Related Jobs are Among Fastest-Growing," *The New York Times.* New York: New York Times Company, March 24, 1985, Section 12, p. 50.

Rudolph, Barbara. "Dropping the Other Shoe," *Time.* Los Angeles, CA: Time Inc., September 9, 1985, p. 54.

S

Sabelhaus, John E., and Bednarzik, Robert W. *Earnings Losses of Displaced Workers,* U.S. Department of Labor. Washington, D.C.: GPO, January 1985.

Samuelson, Robert J. "Job Fears and Facts," *National Journal.* Washington, D.C.: Government Research Corporation, June 25, 1983, p. 1348.

Samuelson, Robert J. "U.S. Industry Will Survive," *The Washington Post.* Washington, D.C.: The Washington Post Company, June 19, 1985.

Sawhill, Isabel V. "Rethinking Employment Policy." Washington, D.C.: The Urban Institute, October 1985.

Schoepfle, Gregory K. "Imports and Domestic Employment: Identifying Affected Industries," *Monthly Labor Review,* Bureau of Labor Statistics, U.S. Department of Labor. Washington, D.C.: GPO, August 1982.

Shultze, Charles, L. "Industrial Policy: A Dissent," *The Brookings Review.* Washington, D.C.: The Brookings Institution, Fall 1983.

Serrin, William. "Engineering: Outlook is Rewarding in Most Specialities," *The New York Times.* New York: The New York Times Company, March 24, 1985, Section 12, p. 21.

Serrin, William. "'High Tech' Is No Job Panacea, Experts Say," *The New York Times.* New York: The New York Times Company, September 18, 1983, Section 1, p. 1.

Serrin, William. "Imports Bill Illustrates Difficulty of Protecting Jobs," *The New York Times.* New York: The New York Times Company, December 6, 1985, Section B, p. 28.

Serrin, William. "Part-time Work New Labor Trend," *The New York Times.* New York: The New York Times Company, July 9, 1986, p. 1.

Shabecoff, Philip. "Labor Board Eases Way for Company Shifts," *The New York Times.* New York: The New York Times Company, January 25, 1984, Section A, p. 1.

Shank, Susan E., and Getz, Patricia M. "Employment and Unemployment: Developments in 1985," *Monthly Labor Review,* Bureau of Labor Statistics, U.S. Department of Labor. Washington, D.C.: GPO, February 1986.

Silk, Leonard. "Automation's Labor Impact," *The New York Times.* New York: The New York Times Company, January 8, 1986, p. D-2.

Silvestri, George T., and Lukasiewicz, John M. "Occupational Employment Projections: The 1984-95 Outlook," *Monthly Labor Review,* Bureau of Labor Statistics, U.S. Department of Labor. Washington, D.C.: GPO, November 1985.

Simmons, Nicole. "Research and Development: A Record Pace," *The New York Times.* New York: The New York Times Company, March 24, 1985, Section 12, p. 8.

66

Stone, Charles F., and Sawhill, Isabel V. "Labor Market Implications of the Growing Internationalization of the U.S. Economy," Draft, June 1986.

Stone, Charles F., and Sawhill, Isabel V. "Labor Market Implications of the Monetary/Fiscal Policy Mix," Testimony before a joint hearing held by The Economic Policy and Human Resources Task Forces of the House Budget Committee, November 1985.

Strategy for U.S. Industrial Competitiveness. A Statement by the Research and Policy Committee of the Committee for Economic Development, April 1984.

"Structuring New Jobs," *The Wall Street Journal.* New York: Dow Jones & Company, Inc., May 18, 1983, p. 34.

Summary of JTLS Data for JTPA Title IIA and III Enrollments and Termination During July-September 1985. Office of Strategic Planning and Policy Development, U.S. Department of Labor. Washington, D.C.: GPO, January 1986.

T

Technology and Structural Unemployment: Reemploying Displaced Adults. Office of Technology Assessment, U.S. Congress. OTA-ITE-250. Washington, D.C.: GPO, February 1986.

Thurow, Lester C. "A Non-Industrial Revolution," *Newsweek.* Los Angeles: Newsweek Inc., January 9, 1984, p. 79.

"Trade Aid Doesn't Stress 'Adjustment'," *National Journal.* Washington, D.C.: National Journal, Inc., January 11, 1986, p. 90.

Trends in Manufacturing: A Chartbook, Bureau of Labor Statistics, U.S. Department of Labor, Bulletin 2219. Washington, D.C.: GPO, April 1985.

Tropper, Peter; Busansky, Alex; and Duggam, Paula. "The Penalty for High Unemployment: Update on Unemployment Insurance Issues," Washington, D.C.: Northeast-Midwest Institute. August 1983.

Tugend, Alina. "Job-Training Act Failing Youths, Analyses Find," *Education Week.* Washington, D.C.: Editorial Projects in Education, January 23, 1985.

U

"United States-Japan Comparative Study of Employment Adjustment," U.S. Department of Labor, Bureau of International Labor Affairs, March 1985.

Urquhart, Michael. "The Employment Shift to Services; Where did it Come From?" *Monthly Labor Review,* Bureau of Labor Statistics, U.S. Department of Labor. Washington, D.C.: GPO, April 1985.

V

Vroman, Wayne. "Innovative Developments in Unemployment Insurance," Research Report Series, RR-85-02. Washington, D.C.: National Commission for Employment Policy, Feburary 1985.

Vroman, Wayne. "Unemployment Insurance Financing: Problems and Prospects." Washington, D.C.: The Urban Institute, February 1985.

W

Wachter, Michael L., and Wascher William L. "Labor Market Policies in Response to Structural Changes in Labor Demand," Department of Economics, University of Pennsylvania and Board of Governors Federal Reserve System, August 1983.

Walker, Gary et al. "An Independent Sector Assessment of the Job Training Partnership Act," March 1984.

Weidenbaum, Murray L. *Imports and Unemployment: Dispelling the Myths.* St. Louis: Center for the Study of American Business, Washington University, October 1985.

Weinberg, Edgar. *Employment Security in a Changing Workplace,* Work in America Institute Studies on Productivity. New York: Pergamon Press, 1984.

Weitzman, Martin L. *The Share Economy: Conquering Stagflation.* Cambridge, MA: Harvard University Press, 1984.

Wintner, Linda. "Employee Buyouts: An Alternative to Plant Closings," Research Bulletin No. 140. New York: The Conference Board.

"What a Way to Make a Living," Special Report, *National Journal.* Washington, D.C.: National Journal, Inc., July 27, 1985, pp. 1724-25.

OBJECTIVES OF THE COMMITTEE FOR ECONOMIC DEVELOPMENT

For over forty years, the Committee for Economic Development has been a respected influence on the formation of business and public policy. CED is devoted to these two objectives:

To develop, through objective research and informed discussion, findings and recommendations for private and public policy that will contribute to preserving and strengthening our free society, achieving steady economic growth at high employment and reasonably stable prices, increasing productivity and living standards, providing greater and more equal opportunity for every citizen, and improving the quality of life for all.

To bring about increasing understanding by present and future leaders in business, government, and education, and among concerned citizens, of the importance of these objectives and the ways in which they can be achieved.

CED's work is supported strictly by private voluntary contributions from business and industry, foundations, and individuals. It is independent, nonprofit, nonpartisan, and nonpolitical.

The two hundred trustees, who generally are presidents or board chairmen of corporations and presidents of universities, are chosen for their individual capacities rather than as representatives of any particular interests. By working with scholars, they unite business judgment and experience with scholarship in analyzing the issues and developing recommendations to resolve the economic problems that constantly arise in a dynamic and democratic society.

Through this business-academic partnership, CED endeavors to develop policy statements and other research materials that command themselves as guides to public and business policy; that can be used as texts in college economics and political science courses and in management training courses; that will be considered and discussed by newspaper and magazine editors, columnists, and commentators; and that are distributed abroad to promote better understanding of the American economic system.

CED believes that by enabling businessmen to demonstrate constructively their concern for the general welfare, it is helping business to earn and maintain the national and community respect essential to the successful functioning of the free enterprise capitalist system.

HONORARY TRUSTEES

STATEMENTS ON NATIONAL POLICY ISSUED BY THE RESEARCH AND POLICY COMMITTEE

SELECTED PUBLICATIONS

Work and Change: Labor Market Adjustment Policies in a Competitive World *(1987)*

Leadership for Dynamic State Economies *(1986)*

Investing in Our Children: Business and the Public Schools *(1985)*

Fighting Federal Deficits: The Time for Hard Choices *(1984)*

Strategy for U.S. Industrial Competitiveness *(1984)*

Strengthening the Federal Budget Process:
A Requirement for Effective Fiscal Control *(1983)*

Productivity Policy: Key to the Nation's Economic Future *(1983)*

Energy Prices and Public Policy *(1982)*

Public-Private Partnership: An Opportunity for Urban Communities *(1982)*

Reforming Retirement Policies *(1981)*

Transnational Corporations and Developing Countries: New Policies for a
Changing World Economy *(1981)*

Fighting Inflation and Rebuilding a Sound Economy *(1980)*

Stimulating Technological Progress *(1980)*

Helping Insure Our Energy Future:
A Program for Developing Synthetic Fuel Plants Now *(1979)*

Redefining Government's Role in the Market System *(1979)*

Improving Management of the Public Work Force:
The Challenge to State and Local Government *(1978)*

Jobs for the Hard-to-Employ:
New Directions for a Public-Private Partnership *(1978)*

An Approach to Federal Urban Policy *(1977)*

Key Elements of a National Energy Strategy *(1977)*

The Economy in 1977-78: Strategy for an Enduring Expansion *(1976)*

Nuclear Energy and National Security *(1976)*

Fighting Inflation and Promoting Growth *(1976)*

Improving Productivity in State and Local Government *(1976)*

*International Economic Consequences of High-Priced Energy *(1975)*

Broadcasting and Cable Television:
Policies for Diversity and Change *(1975)*

Achieving Energy Independence *(1974)*

A New U.S. Farm Policy for Changing World Food Needs *(1974)*

Congressional Decision Making for National Security *(1974)*

*Toward a New International Economic System:
A Joint Japanese-American View *(1974)*

*Statements issued in association with CED counterpart organizations
in foreign countries

CED COUNTERPART ORGANIZATIONS IN FOREIGN COUNTRIES

Close relations exist between the Committee for Economic Development and independent, nonpolitical research organizations in other countries. Such counterpart groups are composed of business executives and scholars and have objectives similar to those of CED, which they pursue by similarly objective methods. CED cooperates with these organizations on research and study projects of common interest to the various countries concerned. This program has resulted in a number of joint policy statements involving such international matters as energy, East-West trade, assistance to the developing countries, and the reduction of nontariff barriers to trade.

CE	Círculo de Empresarios Serrano Jover 5-2° Madrid 8, Spain
CEDA	Committee for Economic Development of Australia 139 Macquarie Street, Sydney 2001, New South Wales, Australia
CEPES	Europäische Vereinigung für Wirtschaftliche und Soziale Entwicklung Reuterweg 14,6000 Frankfurt/Main, West Germany
IDEP	Institut de l'Entreprise 6, rue Clémont-Marot, 75008 Paris, France
経済同友会	Keizai Doyukai (Japan Committee for Economic Development) Japan Industrial Club Bldg. 1 Marunouchi, Chiyoda-ku, Tokyo, Japan
PSI	Policy Studies Institute 100, Park Village East, London NW1 3SR, England
SNS	Studieförbundet Näringsliv och Samhälle Sköldungagtan 2, 11427 Stockholm, Sweden